THE QUAILS

THE MACMILLAN COMPANY
NEW YORK • BOSTON • CHICAGO
DALLAS • ATLANTA • SAN FRANCISCO

MACMILLAN AND CO., LIMITED
LONDON • BOMBAY • CALCUTTA
MADRAS • MELBOURNE

THE MACMILLAN COMPANY
OF CANADA, LIMITED
TORONTO

THE QUAILS

By

Edward S. Spaulding

ILLUSTRATED BY FRANCIS LEE JAQUES

THE MACMILLAN COMPANY

NEW YORK: 1949

First Printing

PRINTED IN THE UNITED STATES OF AMERICA

THIS BOOK IS DEDICATED TO

THE BEST QUAIL HUNTER I KNOW

John Stevenson Edwards

TABLE OF CONTENTS

ILLUSTRATIONS

PREFACE

The purpose of this volume is to bring together in convenient form for the sportsmen of America brief accounts of the seven species of Quails native to the United States. Obviously, a knowledge of the habits and color patterns of the various species in the group will increase the hunter's appreciation of the particular quail that he finds in his locality.

In the illustrations that follow, the cock is presented in one position so that each will be compared with the others easily and understandingly. The excellence of the illustration speaks for itself, and stands in need of no further comment or praise by the author.

The California Valley Quail, that fine game bird about which so many hunters know little, has been used in many instances as a basis for comparisons. In at least two instances unsuccessful hunts have been described in detail. In the case of the Mearn's Quail, not to include the description of a blank hunt would be wrong for the simple reason that most Mearn's Quail hunts are unsuccessful hunts.

Those readers who wish for more detailed information about the Bobwhite should read that great book, "The Bobwhite Quail," by Herbert Lee Stoddard. Those who wish for close descriptions and accurate charts of the three California Quails will find these in Joseph Grinnell's "The Game Birds of California," and in William Leon Dawson's "Birds of California." J. Stokley Ligon is the authority on desert forms.

To show clearly the relationships existing between the different quails mentioned in the text, a chart has been made on which the birds appear in the places assigned to them by James Lee Peters. Above the scientific name of each species appears the field name. In choosing field names for the different races or subspecies, it is common practice for the sportsman to use geographical designations. In the case of the Bobwhite, for example, it is customary to speak of the "northern" race, the "southern" or "Florida" race, or the "Texas" race. On the chart this reasonable practice has been followed throughout. With the genera, however, there is no such common practice; indeed, there are no field names whatever used by sportsmen to designate these groups. New names, therefore, have had to be found. Wherever possible, the English equivalent of the Latin name has been used. Where this has not been practicable, as has happened in some cases (*Callipepla*, for example, means "beautiful dress"), new and, I hope, appropriate names have been set down.

EDWARD S. SPAULDING
Santa Barbara, California

Chart of Quails Mentioned in Text

RACE	SPECIES	GENUS	SUBFAMILY	FAMILY	ORDER
Northern (*brunnescens*)	Valley (*californica*)	Topknotted Quails (*Lophortyx*)	New World Quails (*Odontophorinae*)	Quails & Partridges (*Phasianidae*)	Fowls (*Galliformes*)
Southern (*californica*)					
Catalina (*catalinensis*)					
Western (*gambelii*)	Desert (*gambelii*)				
Olathe (*sanus*)					
Yaqui (*bensoni*)	Elegant (*douglasii*)				
Blue (*pallida*)	Scaled (*squamata*)	Crested Quails (*Callipepla*)			
Chestnut-bellied (*castanogastris*)					
Northern (*picta*)	Mountain (*picta*)	California Mountain Quails (*Oreortyx*)			
Central (*palmeri*)					
Southern (*confinis*)					
Border (*mearnsi*)	Massena (*montezumae*)	Aztec Quails (*Cyrtonyx*)			
Sonoran (*montezumae*)					
Masked (*ridgwayi*)	Bob White (*virginianus*)	Upland Quails (*Colinus*)			
Eastern (*virginianus*)					
Southern (*floridanus*)					
Western (*texanus*)					
Mediterranean (*coturnix*)	Migratory (*coturnix*)	Continental Quails (*Coturnix*)	Old World Quails & Partridges (*Phasianinae*)		
English (*perdix*)	Gray (*perdix*)	Partridges (*Perdix*)			
Italian (*italica*)					
Hungarian (*perdix*)					
French (*rufa*)	Red Leg (*rufa*)	Cocks (*Alectoris*)			
				Turkeys	
				Grouses & Ptarmigans	
				Pheasants	

Based on *Check-List of Birds of the World* by James Lee Peters.

THE QUAILS

1

THE QUAILS

Sportsmen recognize seven kinds of quails in the United States. Ornithologists, governed by their own carefully worked out systems of classification, recognize five genera, seven species, and nearly twenty races. Both groups agree that this country was supplied with an extraordinarily abundant number and variety of birds. In the East and South, as every quail hunter knows, is the Bobwhite. Along the Mexican Border are the Scaled or Blue Quail, the Massena Quail, which often is called the Fool Quail, and the Masked Bobwhite. In California are the Desert Quail, often called the Gambel's Quail, the Valley Quail, and the Mountain Quail.

The birds in each of the seven groups differ sufficiently in plumage and habits and calls from those in the other groups to be recognized at a glance by every hunter. Yet their likenesses to one another are even more noticeable than their differences, and by these the family is bound together by the closest ties. All of them, for example, are ground birds that walk about over their differing ranges and that resort to trees during the sunlit hours only when badly frightened. They are all small, averaging about eleven inches in length; and in shape they are round or nearly so. Their wings are round and short and heavily concave, their tails are short and strong and tapered when closed to a rounded point, and their bills are heavy and hard. As may be expected in a sturdy ground fowl, their legs and toes are extraordinarily strong.

In color pattern these quails have certain noticeable markings that are more or less common to the group as a whole. The handsome shield on the throat, for instance, is sometimes white, framed in black, as on the Bobwhite; sometimes it is black, framed in white, as on the Valley Quail; and sometimes these solid colors are broken up into heavy bands of different shades, as on the Massena Quail. On the cock of every species, except the Scaled Quail, the shield is a conspicuous part of the bird's color pattern.

In one form or another, the scaling on the breast and sides is found on most birds. In the matter of crests and topknots, that most conspicuous feature of all western quails, there is a wide variation. While some do not possess topknots, all have crests that can be raised or lowered at will. By the positions of these crests many emotions are shown.

The country over, the quails look to about the same sources for food. This food consists very largely of vegetable matter: grasses and clovers and seeds of many kinds. Some animal matter is mixed with this, but not a great deal. All of this is found on the ground, the birds plucking and scratching and picking as they glean forward. The quail scratches first with one foot and then with the other, just as an ordinary hen does; this is very different from the method of the sparrow, who puts more effort and agility into the operation, using both feet held close together at each stroke.

It is pleasant to watch a flock of quail of any species. The birds as individuals forage in a weedy clearing yet all are held together by the covey instinct. While feeding, the birds may be fairly widely scattered, with two or three perhaps well to one side of the main bunch, while four or five may be on the other side. Some are gleaning assiduously; a pair of cocks may squabble briefly over a morsel of food; a single bird may stand motionless with its neck stretched to the utmost as it looks intently at some object that has aroused its suspicion. Usually at such a time there is a great deal of conversation going on among the different birds. This may consist of the loud location call given at intervals first by one individual and then another, or it may be an angry or alarmed sputter. Most likely, it will be a low and constant twitter that is heard only by those ears that are within a few feet of the talking birds. The loud and most often heard calls of the various species of American quails resemble one another to a noticeable degree both as to sound and use.

On the wing the different species look very much alike. One may appear to be a little larger or smaller than another and a little lighter or darker in color; but the flight is about the same in every case. They all rise from the ground, almost seem to explode from the ground, in a great and noisy flutter of wings and attain high speed very quickly; and then they disappear from sight over the hill or behind a tree in a swift and noiseless glide on rigidly held wings.

How fast a quail can fly when hard pressed is not surely known. Each hunter makes his own estimates on this highly controversial question and no two estimates agree wholly except in general that a quail reaches high speed very quickly. My opinion, based admittedly on insufficient evidence, is that they can fly over level land, when pressed, at speeds a little better than twenty-five miles an hour. This, I think, is a very little less than the speed of the Cooper's Hawk, the quail's worst enemy. Accurate observations in this field are so very hard to make, however, that I hold this estimate subject to change at any time on the finding of new data. As one of the bases for this estimate I give the following personal experience:

I was present one morning when a Cooper's Hawk came swinging at speed under the live oaks and put up a flock of robins that was feeding on the wet ground between the trunks. Singling out its victim on the instant, the hawk gave chase and over level ground caught the unfortunate bird in almost two hundred feet from the spot where it had flushed. In this deadly race it should be noted that the robin started from scratch and the hawk from a speed of at least fifteen miles an hour. I have timed the flight of robins many times and I have become convinced that this large thrush flies over level ground, when pressed only moderately, at a speed of a little less than twenty-five miles an hour. I doubt that the average Cooper's Hawk flies much faster than this before it dives on its intended victim from above.

As is the custom of other ground birds and some perching birds, the quails nest on the ground, usually in the protection of some grassy or briary tangle, but not always. Occasionally a nest is found under an overhanging spray or two almost in the open. In general, the eggs of the top-knotted group are brown in color. Some authorities say that this dark speckled or mottled hue is for protective purposes, that is, to match the soil on which the nest is made; but this interesting theory has not yet received final proof. Those of the crested quails are much lighter, some of them being white or nearly so. In shape all quail eggs are more nearly spherical than is the case with those of many other families.

From 12 to 20 eggs may constitute a clutch, although if the eggs are removed from the nest soon after they are laid, as is so often done with confined birds on game farms, it is not unusual for a single hen to lay in a season 125 eggs, or even more than this number. As the fertility of eggs laid in a natural state is very high when compared with that of eggs laid by barnyard hens in a coop, most of them, if not all, which escape molestation during the period of incubation hatch in due time. What percentage of clutches does escape injury and destruction is not known surely, of course; but, if one judges by what information is at hand, it is not as high as the uninformed hold it to be. In good years, perhaps more than one half of the nests are undisturbed until the chicks come forth from their confining shells and take to the field. In very bad years it may be that not 10 per cent of the hens build nests and bring off young.

Every indication points to a high mortality both of eggs and of chicks. For one thing, the very large number of eggs in the clutch itself indicates that the chances are against any one particular egg bringing forth a chick that will live to maturity even though the juvenal period in a quail's life is but a few weeks in duration.

If there is anything in the theory that nature is economical and does not produce more than is necessary to keep the species alive and flourishing, a rather definite ratio can be worked out between the hazards that face the various animals and plants. A condor, for example, in the San Raphael Mountains, lays but one egg to the clutch, and does not lay one every year. From this fact it seems to follow, even though we think that the California Condor is slowly dying out, this one egg has a good chance of producing a chick that will survive to maturity. This deduction seems to be more reasonable when the size and habits of the birds are considered. The condor is a huge bird that feeds on carrion. It nests in remote mountains, and it is not likely that it has many animate enemies other than man. One cannot imagine a skunk or a hawk or a snake attacking this well armed and largest of American birds.

A hummingbird, on the other hand, a creature as small as the condor is large, lays but two eggs to the clutch. Again it is reasonable to suppose that this tiny yet swiftly-flying and pugnacious creature has but few enemies that prey on it successfully. I know of no bird that a hummer cannot rout easily. Its nest usually is placed on the extreme tip of the limb, a place difficult for most marauders to reach, and it is very carefully and effectually hidden. More than this, the period of incubation is very short for the hummer. We can say with some assurance that a hummer's eggs and young are but slightly menaced by anything save unseasonable weather.

A house finch, or linnet, lays five eggs to the clutch, with the possibility of two clutches a year. This bird, being neither large in body nor well armed, has many enemies to face at all times of the year, and especially is this true in the spring when nests are built and fledgelings attempt their first weak flights.

For further comparative purposes, it is interesting to look at another branch of animal life, one whose eggs and young seem to face the maximum in deadly perils, and to note that there are some three hundred thousand eggs in the roe of a shad.

If we take fifteen as an average for the number of eggs in a quail's nest, though this number is likely to be too high for an average, it follows that the quail has but one thirtieth of the hold on life that the condor enjoys, and at best only one third of that possessed by the many-enemied, common house finch.

While these figures cannot be accepted as exact, they do show that the hazards surrounding a pair of quail in the spring of the year are very great. This hard fact is all too amply borne out by every field observation.

Another characteristic common to our quails is gregariousness. During the greater part of every year they move about on their different ranges in as large flocks as the food supply and other factors allow. The advantages of such a communal existence are many and fairly obvious. For one thing, in the midst of a flock, where so many eyes are open wide for the smallest hint of danger, the individual is much less likely to fall into an ambuscade than is the bird that habitually goes through the coverts alone. It is true that this sense of security may tend to make the individual less alert and wary than it would be without it, yet the security is real and seems to be enjoyed.

Another helpful factor is that, when the birds flush together as a flock, with a great and confusing whirring of wings, the attacker is momentarily disconcerted and at a disadvantage. Every quail hunter is familiar with the exciting confusion that always is a part of the covey's rise. All of us, at one time or another, have been so disturbed that, failing to select a single bird for a target, we have fired without aim into the mass of swiftly rising bodies or have failed to fire at all. This momentary confusion must be experienced by many other attackers, even the hawks. Yet I must admit that I never have seen a Cooper's Hawk display the slightest hesitancy as it darted to the attack on a quail. These fierce pirates of the air pursue their intended victims with a singleness of purpose and a determined viciousness that is remarkable; and it is not to be wondered at that the quails live in terror of them.

If the communal form of life has advantages for the quails, it has disadvantages, too. Most creatures that form close associations such as flocks and herds develop group sounds and calls that help to keep them together at times and in situations when visibility is low or altogether wanting. This general rule applies with particular force to quails. These sociable birds have developed a system of calls and other notes, some of them of surprising sweetness and carrying quality, by which they keep each other acquainted not only with their whereabouts, but with the varying and quickly changing moods of the individuals as well. It is a much mooted question how much definiteness of meaning should be attached to these calls and notes. Without attempting to enter this controversial field, it seems that certain generalities can be set forth. Parenthetically, it may be observed here that anyone studying the methods by which an ordinary barnyard hen controls the movements of her small chicks, and how she conducts herself as she goes about the ordinary business of a hen, may reach as satisfactory conclusions about this problem as does the field man when he watches a flock of quail in the brush and weeds day after day during those minutes or hours in which the birds show themselves to him.

It is certain that, although the so-called "location call" of the quails advises the other members of the covey of the exact location of the calling bird, it has other purposes. Often it is given by a bird from the midst of the united flock. The call of the unmated male in the middle of the nesting season tells any ear that is listening that the caller desires a mate. The hen brings her chicks running to her by a distinctive cluck when she has discovered a morsel of food. The "alarm" sputter alerts every member of the covey. When two cocks fight, their angry tones cannot be misunderstood. In addition to these five calls or notes, there are many others, especially a whole series of low chucks and peeps and warbles that can be heard only by ears within two or three feet of the talker. From all this I have come to the conclusion that the quails have the largest vocabulary of any bird known to me.

To the sportsman at least, one of the quails' most attractive characteristics is their gameness. It seems to be a fair question to ask, then, what qualities constitute this gameness in a bird. First of these is, I suppose, that a bird must be wary, it must not be easily come upon; there must be a certain amount of difficulty in the pursuit and capture of it. Quails are wary and wild in the extreme wherever they are much hunted, and they are among the most expert hiders.

A second qualification of gameness is that a bird must be a fast flyer or, if speed on the wing is lacking, must possess some other compensating quality that makes it a difficult target for the sportsman. In this field, too, quails are preeminent, for almost every factor in their flight contributes to this end: the startling whirring of their wings when they spring from the ground, the great speed they are able to attain so quickly, the oftentimes rough and tilted character of the ground over which they fly, and their clever use of tree and shrub as shields around which to swing as the shooter attempts to bring his gun to bear on them—these all make quails peculiarly difficult targets to hit. Anyone who has attempted to shoot the Valley Quail on the steep and brush-tangled hillsides of southern California knows how greatly these four factors enter into the sport.

A third requisite of gameness is that a bird must be able to carry a certain amount of shot without stopping or flinching. The lack of this quality probably more than anything else places the Mourning or Carolina Dove on the very borderline of the game birds in so many persons' minds, if it does not definitely put it across that line and among the non-game birds. The quails have a stronger hold on life than has the mourning dove, even though they cannot approach the latter in speed on the wing. The quails can carry shot.

Of the fourth quality, that of the flavor of the flesh, little need be said here in praise of quails. So famous are they as table delicacies that they have been hunted and trapped for the market, until rigorous legal steps had to be taken to stop this abominable practice which was leading to extermination. Such a high monetary value was put on the quails that in certain localities the professionals all but shot them out completely.

As a game bird and as a so-called "song bird," the Bobwhite undoubtedly is the most famous of this famous family. There are several obvious reasons for this deserved fame. One of these is that the Bobwhite's range is the most extensive of all our quails; it reaches from New England to Texas and Mexico and Cuba. A second is that the eastern and southern part of this range coincides with the section of the United States that was first settled and, therefore, has been hunted for the greatest number of years. More than this, it is the part of the country that holds the bulk of our population today.

Undoubtedly there are more sportsmen who hunt the Bobwhite than hunt all other quails. The fact that hunting dogs can be used to great advantage in shooting the Bobwhite adds greatly to the pleasure that many men derive from hunting this bird. The human race is strongly attached to its dogs, and many a man takes the field with his shotgun for little other satisfaction than that of seeing his dog or dogs at work in weeds and thickets as they quest for these small game birds.

Probably the Valley Quail has the doubtful honor of ranking second in popularity with sportsmen. Certainly the Massena Quail, that little known bird of the Mexican Border, is the least famous and the one that is most seldom hunted. Between these two species must fall the other four quails, the Scaled, the Mountain, and the Desert Quails, and the Masked Bobwhite. If any one of these western quails inhabited a region as fair as Virginia, Carolina, or Tennessee, it is possible that that species would be as well known as is the Bobwhite. This, however, is a matter of pure speculation. As conditions are today, there is no other American quail that compares favorably with the eastern and southern bird in popularity, although the Valley Quail, it seems to me, is more alert and more "game."

With sympathetic interest many poultrymen have watched a hen revel in the luxury of a good dirt bath. Using her strong feet, the hen scratches out a shallow hole in the loose, cool soil. Into this she settles herself; and then, lying first on one side and then on the other, she throws the dirt in showers over her body by a series of short, quick, skillful strokes of her wings. For brief periods between these showers of dirt, she relaxes on the cool earth in evident comfort and pleasure. Occasionally, during such moments of relaxation, the hen rouses herself sufficiently to reach out and with her bill pick up a particle from the ground in front of her.

All the quails enjoy this form of bath fully as much as do the domesticated hens, though it may be only the silent and well-hidden watcher who sees the quail do it. Somewhere in the route taken daily by almost every covey there is an area suitable for sun and dust baths. To these places the quails go with anticipation, and from such places they often come with obvious reluctance. Sometimes this bath area is nothing more extensive than a gopher mound; sometimes it is the cultivated strips between the farmer's vegetable rows; sometimes it is the dust of an old and little-used dirt road. The quails utilize almost any place near cover where bare, loose, and fine soil is to be had. If the birds can find such a place in a well-kept vegetable garden, it is so much the better; for the tender and succulent greens to be taken both before and after the bath are an added attraction.

Usually the covey arrives at its bathing place in a much scattered and strung-out order, and the first comers may finish their toilets before the last of the flock arrives. Many a time an individual bird becomes so absorbed in the pleasures of the bath that it allows the rest of the covey to go off unnoticed. When at last the relaxed quail becomes conscious of its isolation, it gets quickly to its feet, shakes itself thoroughly, and runs off in haste after its departed comrades.

The average farmer looks with some understandable hostility on any agency that is inimical even in the smallest measure to the well-being of his crops. He likes to have the quail about, as a general thing, for he is as conscious of their attractiveness as is the next man; yet he must keep his vegetable garden in order. Sometimes the small depredations of the quail annoy him out of all proportion to the actual damage done because the seeming injury, holes in the mulch, ragged leaves on the lettuce heads, and other minor damage is so apparent. The result often is that the quail are shot, especially if the covey "using" the garden is a large one.

This brings up the whole subject of man's relation to the quails. It becomes evident at once that he is the bird's archenemy. Tens of thousands of the birds are killed every year by hunters. If these were the only losses, tremendous though they are, perhaps the quail populations would not suffer too greatly; certainly they could stand such depredations if given a little protection from other types of loss. However, the curtailment in quail population through hunting is not the only one, nor the greatest. Generally, quail flourish best on land that is most suitable to farming. It is a mistake to suppose that they find as favorable a habitat on poor and barren soil as they do on rich soil. They like best, as does the farmer, the well-drained bottoms and the open, rolling, fertile hills. Two or three species have come to live in mountainous or desert regions, it is true, where farming is difficult or almost impossible. Even here, however, the birds prefer the areas which are most favorable from a human point of view for their habitats. And so it happens that when land is broken and crops planted, the quail that once used these acres for a range are displaced permanently and completely. From how many districts throughout its wide range the Bobwhite has been driven by the plowman! And so it becomes apparent that the plow may have been an even deadlier weapon against the quails than the shotgun, though the latter has certainly been deadly enough.

Not so many years ago numerous well-informed men believed it impossible to raise quail in coops in large numbers. We know now that this is not true. Domestication and semi-domestication, that fond dream of so many sportsmen whose powers have begun to wane or whose opportunities to go into the hunting field have been curtailed, is an accomplished fact. Many states maintain game farms where quails are hatched and raised every year in large numbers. There are privately owned game farms, too, where most of our species of quails can be bought at moderate prices.

In general, the problems that confront the would-be breeder of quail are similar in many instances to those that are faced by the poultryman: the quail require about the same care, they eat mostly the same foods, and they are victims of practically the same diseases. There are, however, two important differences. One is that whereas the barnyard hen is a heavy nonflyer, requiring only side walls to its coop, the quail is small and active and is an expert flyer; and so requires a top to its cage. The other major difference lies in the relative sizes of the two fowls. As an article of diet, however choice, the quail is so small in size that it will serve but one person, and that skimpily. The hen, which is much less trouble to raise, is large enough to serve four, five, and even six people. Economically, then, the quail cannot compete with the hen.

Although full domestication of the quails still lies in the future, semi-domestication already is achieved. Today the bird lover can buy birds of the species that does best in his locality and, liberating these in his garden, can maintain a flock about his house. Usually the conditions found in an ordinary garden are ideal for a small covey of quail. What such a garden lacks in seed foods can easily be compensated for by planting the proper peas and grasses, or by scattering food regularly. Only one danger is likely to threaten this idyllic arrangement, and this is the ordinary house cat gone wild. Against the small and always bird-hungry carnivora the quails are largely helpless. The cat is small enough to go into the grassy and leafy runways and paths, and there it lies in wait for the quail. It is an expert stalker and pouncer. It is quick enough to spring on the quail, especially the young ones, while they are more or less entangled by the cover, and to seize them before they can make off. One such cat in the neighborhood can easily destroy, in a short period of time, the whole covey that has been planted and nurtured with such care.

Were it not for these hunting house cats and their progeny, the quails probably would flourish amazingly in the residential districts of our towns and cities; and this without much aid from the citizens. With the cats in possession of the garden coverts, the quail have but the slightest chance to perpetuate their kind successfully, and, if planted, they quickly disappear.

A flock of quail on the lawn and in the shrubbery is a delightful addition to any garden. To the sportsman and the bird lover such a covey will bring, in all probability, as much or more joy than will any bed of flowers. It will be in bloom, as it were, all the year round. The birds will become tame and confiding. And their cheery calls will wake their owner in the morning to memories of many a fine day spent in the open, rolling, pleasant country that is the home of these beautiful and courageous birds.

2

THE VALLEY QUAIL

Lophortyx californica

The Valley Quail is a sportsman and a gentleman. He goes about from place to place over the sage-covered canyon sides and across the weed-grown bottoms with his topknot held jauntily over his forehead and his bright eye ever on the lookout for trouble. If one of his kind, or any other bird his own size, for that matter, seems to impose upon him, he will stop and fight it out there and then. If the other bird is too large for him, he will rise with a brave whir of wings and glide off to another part of his estate, jaunty and cocky even in retreat.

This quail's day does not begin as early as does that of most birds of southern California. When the first signs of the coming day appear on the eastern horizon, the towhee and the thrasher become restless on their perches in the thick bushes. Before it is light enough to see it clearly, the dove is on the wing. But not so with the quail. He rises long after dawn has come. When the eastern sky begins to turn from white to orange, he may rouse himself and cluck a little; he may even on rare occasions climb to the top of a high branch and send his call forth to greet the rest of the risen world, but it is not until almost sunup that he leaves the brush immediately around his roost and starts out on his daily promenade. Should you chance to meet him at such a time, you will see him with the rest of his covey spread out in open order and traveling casually in a more or less predetermined direction, for each day the flock covers about the same route that it traveled over on the preceding day. There is no definite formation in which the band goes, nor is there any definite leadership; each bird runs or walks here or there as it chooses or as influenced by the actions of another bird. Some run forward with the van, some linger in the rear, but all move forward in the same general direction. So they go through the low, open sagebrush and glean as they go.

Presently, when the sun is well up and the cool of the early morning has dissipated, they will come to a dusty area, and here the whole covey will pause long enough for the birds to take thorough baths.

Sometimes it happens that a covey's range consists of two distinct and well-separated foraging areas. When this is the case, the quail usually make the journey from area to area on foot and in some haste. This was true of a good-sized flock that I hunted year after year in a canyon some miles to the west of my home. The birds roosted in some young oaks on a knoll at the edge of a patch of sage, and each morning they fed through the brush on that side of the canyon. Then, more or less at the same time each morning, they would venture out of the cover and run down into the canyon bottom where there were oaks, sycamores, alders and willows; and, crossing the boulder-strewn creek bed, they would hurriedly run up the hillside and into the sage above. In the evening they made the return trip, often on the wing, to the roosting trees. Usually, these birds were found on the eastern side of the canyon in the morning, and on the western side in the afternoon. Another covey, which lived in a canyon a few miles to the west, exactly reversed this schedule. On those days that they crossed the creek bed, they fed in the morning on the western side of the canyon and in the afternoon on the eastern.

After filling their crops in the morning the quail usually like to go to some convenient, shady place that is well sheltered by overhanging, tangled stems, and there spend a few hours in quiet idleness. At times they drowse, occasionally one or another summons enough energy to cluck and call in a half-hearted way, but much of the time they do nothing at all. During this sleepy period, a bird may perch on a thick branch of a shrub a foot or more above the ground, or it may rest on the ground itself. If its diet that day has been a juicy one, or if it has drunk earlier in the morning, it may be at that moment in no need of water. Generally speaking, these birds drink but little. When the mood for activity strikes them again, the members of the covey rouse themselves, stretch widely, and start on the remaining half of their circuit. Dusk finds them in the neighborhood of their roosting tree. Suddenly they run together; there is a whir of many wings, a rustling of many leaves, and a few excited chirpings, and then there is quiet, for the flock has settled for another night.

Almost any dense tree will do for a night roost for these hardy birds. Unlike many of the other species, the Valley Quail roosts high above the ground. Young, thrifty oaks are most frequently chosen, though a similar tree will serve if a satisfactory oak is not handy to the flock. The olive tree, that serves many species of birds for many purposes, does very well as a quail roost, particularly if planted in close rows so that the foliage grows together in thick masses. In three different locations I have found quail resting in lowly willows, weak and relatively open trees though they were. From this I take it that the quail do not find owls particularly troublesome at night.

Thus life passes for the Valley Quail, with one day very like the next insofar as its prearranged schedule is concerned. Occasionally it changes its feeding grounds, but not often. In the summer and early fall its food is largely seed, tiny particles picked up one at a time, and an insect or two; and so this bird frequents the sage-covered bottom lands where seeds are plentiful and where good cover is always at hand. Sometimes it ventures out into the clumps of dead mustard stalks, but this is not its favorite feeding ground. If it is flushed here, it will take the shortest route back to the friendly sagebrush; or, if its fright is very great, it will go into the dense oak trees.

When the winter rains set in and the grasses and clovers spring up in the clearings on every hillside, the quail changes its diet and for some time lives largely on these tender greens. At this time of year it will not be seen in its former haunts, and its friends and enemies, missing it, may think that it is gone for good. But this is not so. The bird merely has moved out of the wet bottoms and has gone to higher and better drained ground. When the season changes again and late spring turns to summer, it will appear once more on its old range.

In the spring, of course, all former flock habits are set aside. Now each quail pair goes off by itself, the birds scattering widely over the land. At this time of year they become almost friendly with man, their worst enemy, and commonly choose their nesting sites close to his home. Some people believe that they do this because there are fewer natural enemies around an inhabited house than anywhere else in the whole countryside. Certainly this holds for the fox, the skunk, the wildcat, the hawk, and the snake. Although these animals are not there to molest the nesting birds, the house cat is, and it is an even more effective hunter of old and young quail than the others.

The site for the nest is cleverly chosen. For weeks a pair of quail may be in the neighborhood, may in fact be seen every day, yet the nest will remain hidden from all eyes. Sometimes from a vantage point of a rock, a post or an elevated limb in the close vicinity of a nest, the cock will give a one-syllable call. This call, very different from his usual cheery three notes, tells the initiated that his mate has chosen her nesting place and may be even then brooding a part, at least, of her large clutch of eggs. Though you search carefully, chances are you will not find the nest; however, you may come upon it when it is farthest from your thoughts. Usually the nest is on the ground in a deep tangle of grass, weeds and briers, often beneath a pile of brush or dead cuttings. Rarely is it in the grass and vines directly against a house.

While other members of the quail family, the Bobwhite for example, often construct coverings or canopies of grass and small weeds over their nests, the Valley Quail seldom does. One nest that I found in the upper Santa Ynez Valley had such a canopy, but only one. This nest had been built in low grass on the almost level floor at the mouth of Blue Canyon. There were very few bushes here, most of the cover being composed of twelve-inch grass and weeds that grew rather sparsely over the flat bottom. Walking through this grass one day in May, I almost stepped on the nest. As my foot came down, the hen quail jumped from the nest and was away on the instant. I discovered the eggs in a slight hollow in the ground. The canopy was composed of dry stems woven together sufficiently to hold its shape, yet it had a very fragile and weak appearance.

The young appear late in spring, sometimes long after most of the fledglings of other species have left their nests and have learned to take care of themselves, or have fallen prey to one of their numerous enemies. At first the chicks are helpless little puffs of down not much larger than acorns, and at this time many of them must perish miserably. In my younger days, when I came across such a family I used to follow it, watching to see what the little fellows did. Once I deliberately jumped into their midst and stood there motionless to see what would follow. Every baby quail froze on the instant, and I could not see one of them. Then, in less than sixty seconds, one stirred and peeped, then another, and then another. Had I been a cat, I could have caught and devoured every one of that entire family. Sometimes I used to catch and hold them in my hand for a moment before letting them go again. Eventually I realized that after such an adventure not all of the little chicks found their mother; often the rest of the family would hurry off and not know that the one or two chicks were missing, and so I no longer handle any of the chicks. Now when I inadvertently come upon a family of tiny quail or even a nest, I retreat just as promptly and as quietly as is possible. In so doing I hope to make partial amends for my former inexcusable curiosity.

That the newly hatched chicks are in constant danger is shown by the few that survive to become adult birds. Normally, well over a dozen chicks hatch from each clutch of eggs; eighteen or twenty is not an unusual number. Yet it is the usual thing to see only four or five half-grown birds with their parents six weeks later. One morning a woman in Santa Barbara was lucky enough to see a mother and father quail and fifteen chicks walk hurriedly across her lawn to the shelter of the shrubs along the fence. Several hours later, however, she heard a commotion in her garden and, going out there, found the two adult birds sputtering on a low shrub, and under the shrub was her own house cat. Not a chick was in sight. And each morning thereafter, at about the same time of day, that desolated pair of quail, without a single chick following, walked across her lawn, picked a blade here and there, and disappeared into the shrubbery on the opposite side.

Although the chicks are helpless for the first day or two, they rapidly become able to fend for themselves and to avoid their enemies. Were it otherwise, there would be no quail in the world today. In two weeks they can fly a very little, and in two months the flock instinct begins to reassert itself. By midsummer the flocks are more or less permanently formed once more. By October the young birds can hardly be told from their parents.

In the nesting season the observant eye sees many more cocks than hens. This is natural enough, for the simple reason that the hens are on the nests. But this is not the only reason. Even as late as July, I have occasionally seen cocks that appeared to be unmated. This raises the question of the balance between the sexes, and of the reason for the seeming preponderance of males. If these birds were polygamous, it would be a matter of indifference whether there were more females than males; but where the birds pair and go off by themselves to nest, the question of a greater number of males than females is one of some interest. It is one, however, that is not easily answered by the ordinary hunter and farmer. There are many flocks of quail, but it is extraordinarily difficult to count accurately any fair-sized flock as it goes about its daily routine.

One band that I did succeed in counting to my own satisfaction (for I checked each bird as it passed a certain tree bole) consisted of forty-two males and thirty-seven females. This, of course, was only a small band. One incomplete setting of eggs, which was found in the field, and which was hatched under a bantam hen, produced five males and three females. Most hunters agree in the rather indefinite opinion that of the bags that they have brought in from the hunting field, some contained more females and some more males, and that it is probable that the latter bags were the more numerous. Judging from all the information available, it seems that there are a few more males in each flock than females, and that, therefore, a few of these handsome swains—from five to ten out of every hundred birds—must go unmated each year.

Perhaps many of these cocks who call so loudly from their elevated stands are unmated birds. It may be that the impulse that moves the male to call the long, one-syllable note is one of loneliness rather than joy in the possession of a mate. This theory is hardly susceptible of positive proof to the average observer, for whether a nest is found close to a calling bird or not, and usually such a nest is not found, the question still remains an open one. Only the most careful and painstaking observations in the field will make much headway here.

At all times of the year, the male is a gallant appearing fellow with his black throat, gray and lemon breast, and russet waistcoat. His topknot, or plume, is beautiful. The female, though less conspicuously dressed, is a lovely creature, too, in her trim suit of demure Quaker gray. Her topknot is daintier than the male's, and her eye is very bright.

The present latitudinal range of the Valley Quail is extensive, and includes much of the lowlands of California and western Oregon. I, myself, have seen Valley Quail in the very heart of the city of Tacoma, but these came of planted stock. To the south, the Valley Quail's range runs well into Mexico. In altitude, these birds in summer may be found at five thousand feet.

This quail, like most others, is a famous hider and a skillful evader. Given a little scrap of brush—a single twig almost will do—it will escape the eye nine times out of ten. In an oak tree, whether on one of the large limbs or in the twigs and leaves in the outer periphery, it is all but invisible. Once in a patch or tangle of poison oak and young alders, a quail is safe beyond the slightest question. After some birds have been thoroughly frightened, you cannot flush them even though you pass close by the bushes in which they are hiding. A winged bird that falls in the brush may occasionally be recovered by the hunter without the aid of a dog, but the chances are all against such a recovery. As an example of this skill in hiding I give one experience that befell me.

One day I was hunting quail in the Santa Ynez Valley in a particularly steep-sided canyon. I was in the canyon bottom, when suddenly a cock quail, which John had flushed high above me, sailed around the hill well above me and dove almost straight down toward the top of a big oak. How fast this bird was flying I cannot say, but it was at great speed. I fired, of course, not because I expected to be able to hit such a difficult and unusual target, but because, as a boy, I had been trained to shoot at sight. This time I

was luckier than usual—for it was an extraordinarily difficult shot—and I did hit the bird. I hit him but did not kill him, and he landed right side up in an isolated bush. Had he landed in a larger patch of brush, there would have been little chance of my finding him, for the active quail is too expert a hider for me to hope to find without the aid of a dog, and I should have searched for this one but a moment and without expecting to locate him. In this little, isolated bush, however, it seemed as if it were impossible for the bird to find a secure hiding place. And so I walked over to the place where I had last seen him and began my search. At first glance there was no quail visible, which was to be expected; I looked into the bush more carefully. As I still did not see him, I dropped on my knees and began to search systematically and carefully. But, search as I might, I could not find any trace of him. A large rat's nest was on one side of the bush and, failing everywhere else, I began to tear it to pieces. This nest was a large one, almost three feet high and more than four feet in diameter at the bottom; so, though I soon found the entrance hole and worked along this passage, it was some time before I had the nest demolished. Even then I did not find the quail, and I was about to give up in this particular place when, as I turned over the debris of the nest, I noticed the opening of a passage that led under a large, rotten log. Since this seemed to be the only possible place left to explore, I began to uncover this tunnel. I followed it for perhaps fifteen feet, to the end of the log, and there I found my cock quail.

Undoubtedly, the Cooper's Hawk deserves closer scrutiny than is given it by most quail hunters; for, in its natural state, this hawk has done much to shape the habits of the quail. Moreover, oftentimes it is easier for the hawk to locate the coveys than for us. These broad-winged, long-tailed hunters fall on the birds at the most unexpected times, and the quail are never free from the shadow of their wings. Often, when there is a great disturbance in the coverts, when wings whir and voices are raised excitedly, the Blue Darter is the cause of the commotion. If the human observer will freeze in his place and watch steadily, the aerial hunter may be seen as it flies up to an oak after a vain attack and takes station there.

One day I flushed a flock of perhaps two hundred quail at the edge of a barranca on a preserve where there had been no shooting for years. The birds were relatively tame, and since no other enemy was in sight, the covey flew off rather slowly across the field of only a hundred yards' width to the edge of the brush on the hillside above me. As the last one was about to land, a darter fell on this bird's back so unexpectedly and so swiftly that it seemed to me impossible that the bird could escape. Yet escape it did. The quail, not taken unawares as I was, flung itself into the brush and was saved. Having missed its kill, the hawk beat heavily away through the oaks. I could not see where this darter came from so unexpectedly, but I suppose that, on the lookout for quail, it had been perched in an oak tree near by and had taken wing as soon as the bird rose from the ground in front of me.

A friend of mine saw a darter make a similar attack on a covey as the birds flew over a bare field. When first seen, the darter was immediately over the quail and, in this extremity, the latter dropped to the bare ground and crouched there motionless and helpless. My friend yelled his loudest to frighten off the hawk, but he was too far away to do this successfully, and one quail was taken. Enraged by this failure, the man rushed into the house and caught up a twenty-two rifle equipped with a telescope sight. With this deadly weapon he had the satisfaction of knocking the Blue Darter out of an oak a hundred yards away as it devoured its easily-caught prey.

On another day, I was hunting quail in some very rough country and had worked my way fairly into the middle of a small flock of perhaps fifty birds, when I lost contact with them completely. To the uninitiated, such a misadventure would seem to be an impossibility; yet it has happened to me so many times that I have come to accept it as one of the ordinary mishaps of the game. The reason a hunter may lose contact with the birds I suppose, is that a flock of quail, when being shot at, keeps on the move; and it is impossible for the hunter always to know in what direction the birds go. A flock, when first flushed, invariably rises from the ground with a great whirring of wings and goes off in a great curve, more or less intact as a flock. When sufficient momentum has been attained, the birds set their wings and glide downhill at great speed and just above the brush. Usually the hunter is so situated that he sees only the first part of this maneuver, and he falsely assumes that the birds have dropped into the sage not far from the place where he saw them last. This false supposition is very seldom justified, because the birds almost always fly much farther than their low height seems to indicate they will do, and because they run as soon as they come to ground.

Several times, when every condition was favorable for full observation, I have seen Valley Quail glide a full half mile from in front of a companion who had flushed them. Where a clear view of the entire flight is obtained, it is possible, of course, to mark down the spot exactly where they came to ground and to make one's way there quickly enough to keep contact with them. But if a curve of the hill or an oak tree intervenes to shut off one's view, as so often is the case, contact with the birds probably will be completely lost. When this happens, the hunter usually does not see this flock again that day.

On the day of which I write, I had been in the center of the flock, and then, suddenly and unexpectedly, I had lost the birds. I cast about first in this direction and then that without raising a single quail. I was about to give up and go in search of another covey, when a Cooper's Hawk appeared and flew into an oak tree in a little draw on my left and well away from the place where I was searching. Possessing to the full the hunter's unreasonable hatred for these fellow quail hunters, I at once turned aside from my hunting to finish off this individual hawk before it disappeared over the hill. When I approached the tree, the hawk, wary as are all members of this clan, flew out and away. But it had tarried too long. I brought it down with one well-placed charge of shot. To my great surprise, at the roar of my shotgun, quail rose with a great whirring of wings on each side of the barranca across which I had just fired; again I found myself in the midst of the covey.

This was a curious happening, something surprising and more or less unusual in my experience; yet I think that there must have been many similar incidents that occurred while I was hunting, but that I failed at the time to notice. Intent on the quail only, we have no time to observe other things that go on in the brush about us. And so we sometimes miss entirely the significant attitudes and movements of the lesser wild folk; or, if we do notice them, we fail to fit them into their proper places in the scheme of things on the hillside. Were we to watch the actions of the Blue Darter more carefully, I am confident that we would be more successful in our quail hunting.

A strong flyer, the Valley Quail is also a strong runner. This latter quality makes the bird a deceptive quarry to many hunters. On occasion quail can run unbelievably fast. Usually, however, when they run they go at a moderate and steady pace away from their pursuers. If pressed too closely, they invariably move off uphill. Unless greatly frightened, they will not lie close; and this habit makes it difficult for the hunter to use a dog on them to good advantage. More than this, in the hot and often dusty sage, a dog soon tires and eventually collapses. After this happens, the hunter is forced to follow the birds alone as best he can, pushing his way breathlessly up the steep and rough slopes and slipping and sliding down the sidehills until he, too, tires out. If quail are in front of him, he is likely to press on after them, going higher and higher until his heart is pounding like a trip hammer. Quail hunting in the dry, hot hills of southern California is not an easy sport to follow, and only a man in good physical condition can engage in it zestfully.

An interesting and, from the quail's point of view, a sinister sight that one occasionally sees when going through sagebrush is that of a wildcat moving furtively along a little trail. I have encountered these cats at all times of the day except noon. From this I take it that quail and rabbits are among the chief articles of food of this crafty hunter. Judging from what I have observed of the ways of tame cats in the wilds, it seems that it is rather easy for a wildcat to catch a quail. Walking, as the quail habitually do, through the grass in the little trails and passageways under the black sage and "Old Man," it must be a comparatively simple matter for an active cat to pounce on the birds. Certainly tame cats do this very thing with recurring, deadly accuracy, and a wildcat, though larger, should be a more skillful hunter than is its usually well-fed, domesticated cousin. There is no clear weight of opinion among experts on this point, however. A rancher once told me that he went out of his way to protect a family of wildcats that lived in the canyon above his barn because he thought that the cats helped to keep down the ground squirrel population. In this I think that he was not altogether right, for it seems to me likely that these cats killed as many of his quail, which he also wished to protect, as they killed ground squirrels.

That all quails have a strong body scent is well known. On a still day a good bird dog will catch this scent in the air many minutes after a Valley Quail has flown by. Even though my sense of smell is dull compared with that of almost any other mammal, I have been able to pick up the scent by putting my nose close to the ground where a wounded bird has fallen. If this is true, what must be the reactions of a hunting dog in a like situation? As a young man I took it as a matter of course that our quail invariably roosted in trees because, if they stayed on the ground at night in this hot and dry climate, their strong body odor must betray them to every keen-nosed enemy that passed that way. If this is true, however, how is it that a hen quail can build her nest on the ground with the slightest hope of being able to sit on her clutch of at least fifteen eggs unmolested for the twenty or more days that are required to incubate them, to say nothing of the score of days before this period when she is laying her eggs? Without doubt, some of this immunity from molestation comes from the fact that the hen sits motionless.

Probably other factors are involved of which we know little or nothing. As one considers the matter, one cannot but wonder what is the percentage of nests that do escape detection for the required length of time. Skunks find some, and foxes find others; even snakes must find some nests accidentally. And once a nest is found by one of these enemies, it is lost to the quail. As for the little weasel, he must be death itself to many brooding birds. Most of the nests of the Valley Quail that I have found in the weeds and brush have been located in such close tangles that it would have been impossible for a large animal to get to them without considerable effort and noise; but this observation, I think, is not generally true. Often the quail nest in the middle of grass and weed patches, and even in hayfields. Such nests are less likely to be found by vermin, probably, than are those made close against a boulder, a post or a building wall, for such places are the favorite lurking places of many kinds of predators.

The scientists have divided the Valley Quail of California into at least three races, and there are still others in Lower California. This gives to the bird a great range latitudinally, and plantings have added to its range. One of the three races lives on Catalina Island. Holding in the hand a bird shot there, one can easily see the slight differences in size and coloration that are the bases of race. The bird is a little larger and has less brown on its back than has its relative on the mainland some thirty miles to the east. In the brush of a steep hillside, however, these small differences vanish altogether, and all that the hunter sees is a bird similar in every respect to the ones he has shot elsewhere in California.

One covey of Catalina quail that I watched with particular interest had its range near the mouth of one of the larger canyons of the island. Though I could notice no difference in voice, behavior or color as I followed the birds, the peculiarities of the habitat were evident. The hillsides in the short canyon were very steep and very slippery, and there was no canyon bottom at all—merely a crease where the two opposite hillsides met. Though there was much grass and some brush, trees were few. The whole canyon cried aloud of its lack of sufficient rain. The fact that there were many so-called wild goats on the upper ridges added greatly to the strangeness of the scene. It was a most difficult terrain from the hunter's point of view.

Some say that there used to be ten, a hundred, even a thousand Valley Quail where there is one today. Such estimates as the last one are too high to be accepted as fact, of course. The same exaggerations are heard today when any game is discussed anywhere. That there has been a very great shrinkage in the quail population in the last fifty years, however, there can be no doubt. Year by year, the human population of California has increased. This has meant a steady increase in the number of hunters and the amount of land that has been cleared and planted. Many large coveys have been shot out completely or have been so reduced that they are on the verge of extinction, and most ranges have been either cleared of brush or have been so heavily grazed that only the smallest coveys can exist on them today. A flock of one hundred birds is now considered to be a large flock. Some people claim that when a covey of quail is displaced, it moves to other ranges and there continues its existence. This is not true. When a canyon bottom is turned into farmland, the quail that once lived on it have no second range to which they can emigrate. Their lines are permanently broken; they quickly cease to exist.

There are some reasons to suppose that the destructive forces at work against the quail today are slowing down somewhat. Now that the Valley Quail hunting is cut down almost to the vanishing point, many men are becoming interested in the welfare of the bird. Organized groups of sportsmen are busying themselves and so are game commissions in several states; yet, because many of these men are more interested in building up supplies of alien birds—pheasants of one kind or another, and chukars and Hungarian Partridges, to mention three well-known groups—the native stock has not received the encouragement that it must have if it is to hold its own against the horde of gunners that today are pursuing it.

In captivity the Valley Quail will lay quantities of eggs. There are many records of more than a hundred eggs from a single female in a spring. It is seldom, however, that the hen will sit on her eggs; if these are to be hatched, bantams or incubators must be used.

Cooped together, a number of Valley Quail always exhibit a certain amount of wildness; yet if a single chick is raised by hand, it may become so tame that it actually enjoys the company of man. One of my friends had such a bird, a female. It was so attached to its mistress that it called plaintively for her whenever left alone. When liberated in a room of men and women, it would inspect each part of every person's apparel with the greatest care, flying up to shoulder and lap and pecking inquisitively at every bright bead, spangle and button. This bird laid more than 125 eggs in a single season, all of which were infertile, of course, because the hen had no mate. Thinking to relieve the bird's obvious loneliness, a male was caught and put into her cage but this experiment was not successful. One year this remarkable hen made a determined effort to sit on about thirty eggs. Evidently eggs from a wild nest were placed at her disposal, and these she incubated successfully.

One cold afternoon in late spring not long ago, a friend of mine found seven tiny quail, lying stretched out and apparently lifeless on the driveway before his front door. They had been abandoned by their mother, though not more than a day old. The ants had found them and were swarming over their limp little bodies. Even so, he took them up carefully and warmed them in the oven of his kitchen stove. There, wonderful to relate, three came to life, and began running and cheeping in a lively manner about the oven bottom. Then he heated a bathroom to a temperature of about ninety degrees, and moved the little fellows there until he had time to bring them to me.

Baby quail are little balls of fluff hardly larger than good-sized marbles, and are brown in color with darker stripes on the back. Each one has a tiny beak, two black eyes so bright and lively that one wonders how they stay in the tiny ball of a head, and, even so early in life, there is the suggestion of a topknot. I took over the care of these three gallant survivors, and kept them for six weeks in a homemade incubator, warmed by an ordinary electric light. For food I gave them grated raw carrot and cracker crumbs mixed with a very little charcoal and fine gravel, and they throve amazingly. They never lost their wildness, but neither did they lose their charm for me. Perhaps the two were inseparable. At any rate, they were a brave, hardy trio, true to the instincts of their race. While they never seemed to be as beautiful in a cage as their relatives appeared in the brush, they paid me back in joy a hundredfold for the little care they cost me.

From all this it follows that quail can be raised successfully on farms. And from this it follows again that the bird will not be allowed to go with the Passenger Pigeon into oblivion so long as a few good men wish to keep it alive.

3

HUNTING THE VALLEY QUAIL

As one listens sympathetically to the tales of the old and experienced Valley Quail hunters, it becomes evident that this sport, when it is intelligently followed, may be raised to something of an art, and that the pleasures and satisfactions to be derived from it are considerable. As so many of these men describe it, it was a rough and tumble affair, the sport of the true hunter in excellent physical condition, and not that of the marksman primarily; for the best of shots, if he were not also a good hunter, often came home after a long and weary day in the sagebrush with few, if any, more quail in his bag than he had blisters on his feet. In many areas these primitive conditions are now changed, and refinements have taken their places; but in many others conditions are much as they used to be.

Where the old conditions still prevail, the quail hunter, if he is to get any shooting at all, must learn to tell at sight good quail cover from bad. At first thought, this would seem to be an easy thing to do, for sagebrush is sagebrush wherever found, and quail, from choice, live in it. There are so many other factors that go into the making of good quail cover, however, that a given patch of brush is not always what, at first sight, the novice takes it to be. Some men seem to possess an instinct that guides them more or less infallibly to the right place at the right time; others, though they have sought the Valley Quail consistently for years, occasionally are guilty of the most egregious errors of judgment in their choice of cover through which to hunt.

Once the general hunting area has been determined, the next important decision is where, at that particular time of day, the birds are most likely to be in the acres, or even square miles, of brush that stretch away on either hand. This is very important because, if some nook or corner is not recognized for what it is, a flock of birds quietly resting there may be passed by unnoticed at fifty yards. I remember very well one morning I went up a canyon and over a hill without finding a single bird. Returning after an hour and a half of active tramping, I found the flock within a hundred yards of where I had passed as I started out. At the start of the day's work, a dog is of great value, for, even though his nose may be a relatively poor one, his presence in the brush is sensed by the birds and often sets them to sputtering and scolding excitedly. But as dogs, for one reason or another, are not commonly used in Valley Quail hunting, most hunters rely upon their own senses in locating the birds.

There are several methods of locating the positions of the flocks. Some men push through the brush more or less blindly, uphill and down, beating every piece of cover that lies in their path, until at last a flock is stumbled upon. This method, though it requires a vast expenditure of effort and time, is often highly successful. Another method is to go more slowly and carefully, pausing often to study the lay of the land in detail, and to listen long and intently for the faintest call or sputter of the birds. This second and more leisurely method, while it does not carry the hunter over as much territory as does the first one, makes a more pleasant occasion of the hunt and is likely to be at least equally productive.

Speaking very generally of the ordinary day, one that is neither too hot nor cold, the birds are likely to be found well down on a southeastern slope in the early morning and well up on a southwestern slope in the afternoon. If it is very early in the morning, well before sunup, when the hunter arrives on the field, he had best sit down quietly in some favorable place on the edge of the brush and wait there until the quail have had time to come down from their roosts and to start foraging off through the brush before he attempts to find them. Hunters have walked many a useless and tiring mile before the birds were abroad, and tramped by many a good flock which has remained unseen at this early hour.

At this time of day, too, the birds are likely to be more vocal, if they are undisturbed, than they will be later in the morning, Therefore it is sound practice, even after one flock has been located more or less precisely, to remain quietly seated and, if possible, to locate calling birds of another flock—perhaps on the other side of the wide canyon. Presently, it may even happen that birds of a third flock, one so far up the canyon that the calls from it can be but faintly heard, will be encouraged by the calling of the two coveys relatively close at hand to announce their approximate position to the listener. If the situation does develop in this way, the hunter is assured of continuing sport because, after he has flushed and scattered one covey, he can go on to the next one; then, if he still has energy enough remaining to continue the sport, he can search out the third band.

However, if for one reason or another the birds are mute on the morning that the hunter is afield, it may very well happen that the watcher and listener at the edge of the brush will be able to locate a flock of quail by seeing some of its members as they move about in the tiny clearings and bays, or by catching a momentary glimpse of a bird as it appears briefly above the brush at some spot.

If the morning planned for the hunt turns out to be a wet one, there is little use in searching for quail at all that day, for these birds are very reluctant to leave their roosts and to enter the wet and dripping grass. On several rainy days at about noon I have had the opportunity of watching unobserved as a flock fed through the drenched grasses and low brush. At such times the distaste of the individual birds for the all-pervading moisture was obvious and almost comical. Each sought by the use of every possible method to avoid the wet blades and sprays as it moved rapidly here and there; each was in the utmost hurry to fill its empty crop as quickly as possible and then to get to some relatively dry and sheltered spot. This being the case, there is little sport to be had in hunting over the adobe hills on a wet day.

If it is a cold morning, the birds are likely to be found in grassy openings that the sun will strike and warm soon after it appears in the eastern sky. On such mornings they often remain for some time more or less stationary on the ground, their feathers fluffed out until each bird is almost spherical in shape, before they go off to glean on their regular routes over the hills.

If the morning is warm, the quail are likely to fly down from their roosting trees at a slightly earlier hour than is their usual custom, and to work off at once through the sage. On such a morning, within a couple of hours after starting on their daily circuit, they will fill their crops with seeds and other foods. Then they will move to some relatively cool and shady retreat, a place where they can doze away the hot hours without too great fear of interruption.

Because of this custom, if the hunter appears at the edge of the brush on such a warm morning perhaps a couple of hours after sunup, after the quail have filled their crops, he will do well to search the bottoms of the canyons and what are known to deer hunters as "breaks"—bushy areas at the bases of steep, often bare, cliffs or outcroppings of rock. Such areas as these are much used by both deer and quail at suitable times of the day.

By midafternoon the quail may have moved to the brush about in the middle of some hillside or near the top of the slope, though this rule, like the former ones, is only a generality. Perhaps the best rule for the hunter to follow when he arrives on the field either late in the morning or early in the afternoon is to go where the birds were seen on some previous occasion at a time corresponding with the one in which he now finds himself afield, provided always that the former trip was not too long ago.

Because the food of the quail is composed largely of seeds during a dry fall, the coveys then are most likely to be found in those places where seeds are on the ground in the largest quantities, that is, on or near the canyon floors. Later in the year, after this hard diet has changed to one of greens, the birds should be sought on somewhat higher ground, where the grass is not lush and the drainage is good. A covey may move up from a low, wet range to a higher and better drained one in a single day.

This shift in range I encountered with disastrous results to my bag one fall day when we made an extended trip up the coast to a place called Honda. Here, one fortunate week end, a very large flock of quail was seen by us almost as soon as we entered the hills, and we had a memorable shoot. On this day there seemed to be birds everywhere, and no amount of shooting would drive them far from the brush in which they first were found; so it happened that we were able to go back and forth over this cover again and again, and to pick up a bird or two on each trip.

At Honda the physiography is a little different from that of many other places along this coast. Here the sandstone layers that form the Coast Range rise at a sharp angle almost at the sea's edge. There are short, steep hills, and between these are tiny canyons in which the floors are almost as sandy as the beach itself.

Two weeks after finding this fine flock of quail, we went by train back to this place to try our luck again. This time, however, everything went as badly for us as it had gone well on the earlier hunt. We searched through the brush uphill and down, and we plodded over the wide and weary stretches of sand that lay between the brushy areas on the hillsides without any success. How many difficult miles we walked that day it is not easy to estimate accurately, for the sandy bottoms greatly increased in our minds the distances over which we tramped; but it was very many indeed. And in all that weary way we did not see one single quail, nor did we hear a quail call.

The reason for our lack of success on this day, when we had counted so confidently on a splendid shoot, was simply that between the two expeditions the long summer and fall drought had been broken by heavy rains and, therefore, the quail had shifted their range from the old seed-bearing one to another and higher one more suitable to grass and clover. In spite of our complete lack of success, as far as our bags were concerned, that day had been an instructive one for us, for it had taught us, as only hard experience can teach, that the quail hunter does well to keep his eye on the weather at all times of the open hunting season.

Having considered time of day, time of year, temperature, and all the other factors, the hunter taking the field makes his decision as to what part of the brush he will hunt first, and then he sets off up the canyon. If the day is a fortunate one for him, and if his calculations have been accurately made, he will locate with some exactness the position of a flock of quail. At first he cannot be sure how large this flock is, for at any given time it is usual for only a bird or two to call. What he hears may be a small flock rather widely scattered as it roves through the brush, or a large flock closely bunched together. The question of size need not disturb him unduly, for it is one that no amount of skill in stalking or accuracy of aim can change.

The lay of the land, on the other hand, is of the greatest importance to him, and so he pauses for a moment or two and studies carefully the various approaches to the place where the birds are, so that he may select the most advantageous one. Two factors of the forthcoming rise are known. When disturbed, the birds almost surely will attempt at the start, unless they are already at the bottom of the hill, to fly off downhill. Sometimes, however, when a covey that is near the summit of a hill is approached from below, it will go over the crest and down the other side. The other known factor is that the birds, when flushed, will move out of the light brush and go into the heavy brush if there is such a patch within reach. As it is greatly to the hunter's advantage to prevent both of these maneuvers if he can, he will make every effort to place himself between the covey and the cover out of which he wishes to keep them, and to so approach it that when the birds flush they will keep to the same level on which they have been found. He will do this, if he is wise, even at the expense of a long and difficult circuit and a steep climb through thick brush.

If the covey is first located near the crest of a ridge, the hunter is faced with a nice calculation of chances; for, unless he knows thoroughly the country over which he is hunting, he can only guess at the nature of the cover on the opposite slope, the cover which the birds are likely to make for as soon as they rise. If he has not been over this opposite slope, all that he can surmise about it is that if it is a north slope near the coast it is likely to be covered with a tangle of brush, briars and small oak trees;

for such, as often as not, is the growth found on these hillsides where the sun's rays strike more slantingly than they do on southern exposures and where, therefore, the evaporation is much less rapid. The brush there is likely to be composed more largely of Ceanothus and mountain mahogany and other tough and high-growing shrubs than it is of the low growing and easily penetrated sages and small sumacs. In such a situation, therefore, the hunter may decide to approach the flock from along the crest of the ridge, and to attempt to drive the birds downward. This latter course may not be without its disadvantages, for the bottom of the canyon may be lined with oaks and sycamores and other dense and high cover.

Having studied the ground and the cover, and having made his choice, the hunter begins his approach. If there are two or three in the party, the guns probably will be as nearly in a line as the ground permits, and anywhere from twenty to fifty yards apart. This is the ideal formation, but it is seldom followed exactly. Sometimes, in the excitement of the shooting, particularly when the ground is much broken and individual birds, pairs and trios are being followed, all attempts at a formation of any kind are completely given up, and each man shifts for himself. But when a line of sorts can be kept, it often happens that the middle gun gets the best of the shooting, and that one or the other of the wings gets very little shooting indeed. This usually places a premium on the middle position, in the eyes of the novice. But this is not always the case, by any means; for it often happens that, after the first flurry, the birds work out to the sides and so move out of the path of the center man.

Regardless of which way the birds move, it is usual for the other fellow to seem to get all the shooting or, at least, the best part of it quite irrespective of what position one takes for himself; and so obtaining the middle position need not be a matter of great concern. Then too, the actions of the birds, when at last the hunters do approach them, is seldom the same on any two occasions; sometimes they will rise well out of gunshot and make off over the brush so directly that none of the hunters, whatever his position in the line, will be given the opportunity of a shot. Again, there are times when the birds will move off, keeping persistently on the ground, for some distance before taking wing. When this happens, they may move out entirely from before the center man. Because of this latter tendency, there are occasions when it is both desirable and profitable to drive the birds on the ground for a little way, perhaps to a slightly more favorable situation for the hunter, before flushing them. However, this requires both skill and patience and also considerable time and luck.

Two experiences of mine illustrate this phase of Valley Quail hunting very well. Necessarily they occurred many years apart, for one does not often attempt to drive quail on the ground. The first happened when I was hunting with a companion just out from the East and, at the moment, in rather soft physical condition. This man did not wish to undertake a grueling hunt over the hot, rough hills, and so we had decided to look for birds in low and easily hunted brush. At the start of this hunt, at any rate, luck was with us, for we came on a good-sized flock in the angle where the hillside merged with the canyon bottom. This is a very common place in which to find Valley Quail, for it is the area that receives the greatest amount of water during and after every rain storm and, consequently, often has the richest vegetation. After locating the birds with some exactness, my companion took a position at a favorable place to one side of the birds and at a slightly higher level. I went around the covey in a wide arc and approached them slowly and cautiously from the other side. As soon as they became aware of my presence they began to sputter, but as I was careful not to crowd them, they did not become greatly alarmed. I stood motionless at this distance until, after a few minutes of uncertainty, they began to move off and away from me. Since they continued to sputter as they moved away, I was able to keep accurate track of their progress, and by shifting my position a little this way or that, as the case seemed to demand, I was able to move the whole covey across the area in front of my motionless companion. Because their attention was fixed on me, they did not see him until the van was within twenty feet of him. Then, with a startled note or two, these birds flushed and took the whole covey with them in a strung-out formation. We hailed this drive as a great success, and my confidence in myself as a quail hunter was greatly increased.

Some years after this, when I again attempted to drive a large covey of quail, my self-confidence received a rude setback. At this time I needed a cock Valley Quail for purposes that had nothing to do with hunting, and I went out to the ranch of another friend, an old hunter who knew the habits of the Valley Quail thoroughly, and explained my need to him. He told me of a flock of quail that ranged in the near vicinity of his home during the day and roosted in a Cherokee rose hedge beside his house at night. At the moment, about three o'clock on a warm afternoon, he thought that the covey could be found at a certain place about half way up a small hillside. He was not averse to having one male taken from this garden flock because he knew that one male more or less would make no difference in the continuation of the flock's existence, but he was most skeptical of my ability to select a cock from the confused mass of birds on the covey's rise. This was a nice point, to be sure. I was fairly confident of my ability, however, because it seemed to me that I usually knew the sex of the bird at which I was aiming when I pulled the trigger. My friend doubted this, holding, quite correctly, that while the facial markings of the male were distinctive, the hunter had small opportunity to see them as the birds flew away from him. The topknot, that most distinctive feature of the male, my friend Lawrence said, was held far back on the head when the bird was in flight and so it presented a very inconspicuous mark for the shooter to find in the great excitement and confusion of the covey rise. We argued the matter at some length, as old friends will do, and when at last we both saw that neither could convince the other by argument, we decided to locate the quail on the hillside.

As so often happens when hunting quail, we found the covey exactly where Lawrence had said it would be. The birds were completely hidden from us by shoulder-high brush, and all that revealed their presence was a low note or two that occasionally issued from the sage under which they rested. These sounds could be heard only at a very short distance. Had we been on a regular hunt in strange country, we should almost certainly have walked by these birds, a flock of perhaps seventy-five, without an inkling of their presence unless by sheer luck we had stumbled directly upon them.

Having located the covey, my friend was for walking in on it and then, when the birds came boiling up through the thick, high brush, of letting me prove or disprove my stubbornly held contention with one shot. With the covey immediately in front of me, I suddenly found myself a little skeptical of my previously claimed ability always to select cocks for targets, and I now remarked that it seemed foolish to risk the death of a hen in this garden flock that he prized so highly. I suggested instead that we drive the covey downhill a short way and across a little clearing in the brush, even though I knew that quail dislike to move away from danger downhill. Once the birds started to cross the clearing, I said, it would be a simple matter to select a cock and to kill it. With some reluctance he agreed to this change in procedure. The quail, however, were against the proposal. We spent the next fifteen or twenty minutes, employing every stratagem we knew, in a vain attempt to start the birds. The quail refused to budge from their position in the high sage. At last Lawrence took a step too near, and at this they came boiling up through the sage in a tremendous commotion. A moment before, the entire scene had been quiet and motionless, a still patch of fragrant gray sage on a sleepy, sun-drenched hillside. Now, on the instant, the air was filled with hurtling gray forms and a most exciting roar of sound. To the quail hunter nothing could be more thrilling than this!

Keeping my head as best I could, I selected a bird that seemed to me to be a male. Though it flew in the van and was on the far side of the flock, it was one of the first birds to come into sight, and so I had a good view of it. I fired, and it fell dead. By the greatest misfortune, however, it dropped into a deep barranca choked with blackberry and Ceanothus and, obviously, was lost. I dropped another bird from among the laggards of the fast-disappearing flock. I saw this second bird fall into the thick brush behind the curve of the hill; but, as I was able to mark down an accurate line to the spot where I had last seen it, I anticipated little trouble in retrieving it. And in this anticipation we were not deceived, for, in less than five minutes, my companion located the dead bird. I may as well confess at once that when he held it up to me I felt considerable relief in seeing that it carried the markings of the male bird. Elated by this but half-expected success, I went down to the edge of the barranca and peered over the edge. This was as much a matter of habit as anything else, for I had no hope whatever of seeing my first bird there; yet, on a tiny spot of bare ground no larger than my hat brim, I saw my first-shot bird lying dead. It, too, was a fine cock, and I retrieved it with the certainty that even though the drive had been a complete failure, this was my lucky day.

So much for the correct approach. Once the birds are in the air and are making off as fast as wing and gravity can impel them, it is of the utmost importance to mark down the spot where the largest portion of the covey comes to earth, for it is seldom, indeed, that the whole flock stays together after the covey is flushed and has been fired upon.

The alert hunter will also try to mark the smaller divisions so that he can come back for them after the larger portion has been thoroughly worked and lost, but this is not always possible. If the settling place is in a brush-filled barranca, it is likely that the birds will lie for a little while where they have landed. If it is a lightly covered hillside, they will move off and upward at once. In the latter situation, the hunters must go to this place as fast as they can, and should beat across the hillside and back again at an elevation slightly higher than the one on which the birds landed. Each time the hillside is crossed, it is likely that individual birds and pairs and trios will be put up, even though the hunters retrace their steps exactly; for the birds will continue to work up the hill and, as they do this, they continually cross the paths of the patroling sportsmen. Most of these birds, when put up, will make off away from the approaching gun, giving that man a quick straightaway or an angling shot. About every fifth bird, however, is likely to lie motionless until the hunter has passed the little bush in which it is hiding, and then, getting up, it will go off in a direction opposite to that taken by the other birds. This is a stratagem very disconcerting to the shooter, and many a bird executes it in safety.

If it were on open, level ground where the footing is good, there would be no great difficulty in such a shot, for the noise of the rising bird gives the hunter ample notice of what is happening. But when one is on a steep hillside, where the footing at best is difficult, even precarious, where the free movement of both gun and body is greatly hampered by the entangling brush, and where the bird has but a short space to fly before it is covered by intervening brush or tree or hillside, it is seldom easy to whirl about quickly and fire without losing one's balance and, as a consequence, one's target.

Once a flock is completely scattered, there is little profit for the hunter in wandering at random over the hills in the hope of stumbling upon individual birds whose whereabouts have not been carefully marked down. It will be more profitable to go in search of another flock. If one sits down and quietly waits for the scattered birds to begin to call, as they usually will do in a short while, he may get some idea of the whereabouts of some of the flock, but he will get few shots by trying again for these birds. As a rule, it is the lone bird that calls first, and such singles are very difficult to locate with sufficient exactness to make it worth while to search them out.

But no man, however experienced, can say surely how any given flock will behave when flushed at any given time. Sometimes the birds fly straight away, and when they do this they make easy targets of themselves for even a fair shot. Again they break back in tight semicircles at a height of perhaps ten feet above the top of the brush, and when this occurs even the marksman will have a good opportunity to show his skill with the shotgun. If the shooter is one-sided, that is, if he shoots much better on one side than the other, he will be amazed at the number of birds that go by him on his weak side. Obviously, the quail cannot know one side from the other; yet after two or three have by chance selected for their escape that side which the shooter finds to be the more difficult, it will seem to him that they are doing so with forethought. One bird missed on the weak side makes as deep an impression on the average hunter's consciousness as do three killed on the right side.

One morning, when my friend John and I were hunting near the hamlet of Los Alamos, we came on a huge flock of quail at the foot or point of a long, narrow, and steep-sided ridge that rose higher and higher as the eye followed it to its seeming crest. The whole ridge area was covered with relatively low brush that included most of the varieties of shrub that quail find useful. It was an ideal situation and, if the birds followed their usual tactics of flushing straight away and up (they could not go down in this situation), we were assured of a memorable shoot. John took the left and I took the right as we started forward. The covey flushed with a tremendous whirring of wings and went into the brush in pairs and trios and little groups here, there, and everywhere on the ridge. How many there were it is impossible to state with any degree of accuracy. Five hundred would not be too large a figure, I am sure, and there may have been a thousand birds in that flock. Thrilled by this unusually happy start, we at once followed them into the brush of the ridge.

Many of the birds stayed on the crest of the ridge in front of us, continuing up and up in a series of short flights, and many, on my side at least, worked off sideways into the brush on the steep ridge face. At one point in my progress upward, after I had shot and retrieved a dozen or more quail, I marked down a bunch of three or four dozen birds that jumped up in front of me with others and then, separating from their companions, came to earth well above me and well out on the ridge face. I made a mental note of this location and continued on up the ridge. When I reached what I deemed to be their approximate altitude, I turned off from the ridge crest and went in search of them. Such a quest cannot be made with exactness, of course, because the birds may or may not lie where they land, and because, in the excitement of the shooting that intervenes between the times of seeing them come to earth and of setting out in search of them, one loses one's bearings somewhat.

In this particular case, I was not to know whether I had judged my altitude correctly or not, for, while I was still a little way from the spot where I now supposed that the birds had settled, a cock bird jumped out of a bush at my feet and plunged directly down the slope. I shot him, and he fell dead in the bushes far below me. As I looked down on this cover, it seemed to me that I should have let this bird go unharmed for, while the rest of the hunt was progressing steadily upward, it had chosen an exactly opposite course in which to escape. As long as I had shot and killed him, however, I felt duty-bound to retrieve him, so I slid, slipped and scrambled down the steep, slippery hillside to the place where he had fallen. As I stooped to pick him up, another bird jumped out, almost from under my hand, and in its turn, it went straight downward. Instinctively, before I had time to collect my startled thoughts, I shot and killed this one too, and then I plunged downward once more to retrieve it. It became apparent now that I had become involved in one of those curious, rare, and wholly inexplicable cycles where events happen one after the other with unreasonable consistency. I now was certain that I should have let the first down-plunging quail go unshot. It was too late to withdraw, however, and so I went on slipping and sliding down the ridge side to the place where my second quail had fallen. When I reached this spot, a third bird jumped and went downhill as fast as wings and gravity could drive it. And again, half instinctively, I shot and killed my bird. Again I went down and retrieved my kill. As I straightened up after this third plunge down the steep hillside, I looked back to the top of the ridge. There, on the far skyline stood John. He was waving to me, and I faintly heard him yell that the rest of the covey was getting away from us and that I must hurry back up to my former position.

At this, I started up the very steep side of the ridge as fast as I could go, with the idea of making as much progress as possible before my wind gave out and I should be forced to slow down. Very soon I was panting for breath, and in a few more minutes I was gasping desperately and my heart was pounding furiously. While still a long way from the top of the ridge, I was forced to sit down on a convenient boulder and give my heart an opportunity to slow down to a less dangerous tempo. But even as I rested I heard John call to me again and again, and so, at last, I got up and began to climb the ridge once more.

On this shoot we picked up forty-eight birds, only two less than the day's limit for us. These two remaining birds we collected on the way home, and returned to Santa Barbara with our full quota. When we remembered that on the day before we had bagged our limit of ducks on a fresh water lake in the sand dunes on the coast, near a place called Guadalupe, we considered this our most fortunate excursion in the hunting field. Certainly it was the day that provided for us the so-called ideal quail shoot. I never expect to have another like it.

If, on an ordinary day, the birds when first flushed drop into a narrow, brush-filled barranca, as they so often do when such cover is available, good shooting can be anticipated. With a hunter on either side of the wash, moving slowly forward abreast, the quail come out in singles and pairs and trios, first on one side and then on the other, and offer the hunter sporty targets. Many of the birds flush from their positions on the barranca sides and bottom as soon as the hunters come abreast of their positions, and sticks and stones thrown into their midst dislodge many others that lie hidden in the thickest tangles. Some refuse to be frightened out into the open at the first passage, however, and these birds can be put up later, after the best part of the shooting has been had. Indeed, it is surprising how many times a hunter can return to such cover and still find a bird or two in it.

When the quail are in such a barranca, if the hunters are skillful and fire only after the birds have cleared the brush and trees, there will be little trouble in finding and retrieving those killed; otherwise, many a bird will be knocked down and then lost, or the hunter will find himself continually making trips into the bottom of the brush- and briar-filled barranca. While he smashes his way through this exasperating cover in search of the quail that is down, other quail will burst out, usually from almost under his feet, and will be off through the trees so quickly that he will have no chance for a shot at them.

Sometimes, however, the barranca is both wide and deep—thirty or forty feet in each dimension—with almost sheer sides, and choked with tall willows and alders above and blackberry below. Such a combination is practically unworkable. It is so deep and thickly overgrown on the sides and bottom that the birds cannot be frightened out of it by a man on the bank; and it is so dense, both above and below, that the hunter will get but an occasional snap shot if he tries to force his tortuous way along the bottom through the tangle. More than this, what bird or birds he does succeed in stopping, he will find only with the greatest difficulty. Much more often than not, he will find no trace of them, and there is little profit to be obtained in hunting in a place of this sort, exciting as the shooting in it may be.

These deep and difficult barrancas, however, are at times most compelling in their attractiveness. One may see a large flock of a hundred or more birds, perhaps, dive into these depths and from the security of the upper bank, it appears certain that many shots must follow an excursion after them. I must confess at once that I have spent many an hour in such barrancas. I know of one in particular that I have forced my way into time and time again. The bottom of this barranca is perhaps fifteen feet wide in certain places, and there is a tiny trickle of water over the mud there. Blackberries cover the bottom and sides densely to a minimum depth of perhaps two feet, and fifty-foot willows completely fill its upper spaces. I suppose that I have killed and retrieved less than a half dozen quail in this barranca in all the times that I have followed a flock into its depths. It has always proved to be a hard and profitless venture. Yet, somehow, there always has been enough good mixed with the bad to make me feel that my time there has not been altogether wasted, and to hold out the hope that the next time my luck will be better.

Occasionally a flock of quail is encountered that, for one obscure reason or another, is loath to leave the low sagebrush in which it has been found, and when this happens the shooting is easy. Far more often, however, the birds leave the low brush at once and head for the thickest cover. At such times, if oak trees grow within reach the birds will enter this high cover and lie very close. In this situation they are to all intents and purposes invisible to the hunter. This is rather extraordinary because, on close examination, it will be found that the leaves of our oak trees grow only at the extreme circumference of the tree. This makes a light screen easily seen through when it falls between the eye and the open sky. One might reasonably expect to see bird after bird as they lie here, but this is not the case. As the hunter approaches the tree in which there is a bird or birds, he sees nothing that resembles the round form of a quail, and it is only when a bird bursts through the periphery with a great whir of wings and rustle of leaves that he becomes certain that the tree has, indeed, held a quail. In oaks the quail are apt to land on the larger limbs and to run along these with ease well out to the periphery of leaves, where they come to rest. When they burst out of such a tree they seem to come from a position in the leaves themselves, but, in most instances, this is a false impression. And always, when they go out, they do so on the side opposite the hunter. This common practice makes it nearly impossible to get even the quickest of snap shots at them. Nine times out of ten, they make their escape unseen, a most exasperating experience for the hunter.

A rather unusual experience in this kind of hunting befell me one morning. I was recovering from a severe leg injury, my left leg at the moment being as straight and stiff as the proverbial pine timber, when two of my friends, companions of many a previous hunt, decided to take the field again. Considerately, they invited me to go with them, even though they knew that I could not possibly walk two hundred yards through the brush, to say nothing of the usual five or eight miles. Why I accepted the invitation I cannot say. Perhaps I thought the ride to and from the hunting grounds in such good company would be pleasant. I believe that, at the time, there was some talk of stationing me beside the car on some secluded road at a spot over which the quail might be driven. If this was indeed the case, it was sheer nonsense, for Valley Quail cannot be driven here and there at will. However, I went along with them to the shooting grounds and hoped for the best. When we stopped they went over a rolling hill and left me in the car.

Soon I heard them shooting, and from the timing of these shots I knew that they had come on a fine flock. For a few minutes I stood by the car, listening. Then, unable to stand the strain longer, I took my gun and, working my way through the barbed wire fence as best I could, I went slowly, as my stiff leg demanded, up through the rather open brush and small oaks of a steep hillside in the direction my friends had taken. It was hard work, and I paused often to rest. On one of these rests I saw two or three birds whiz across the open sky far ahead of me. This greatly encouraged me, and I redoubled my efforts. My friends continued to shoot, but no quail came near me. Perhaps fifty yards above the barbed wire fence, I paused for another rest, the climb having proved to be much harder than I had anticipated when I set out. I was pretty well tired out, and remember also that I was greatly discouraged—that it seemed useless to go on. In this frame of mind I surveyed the hillside above me. Then I turned my head to look over the route I had just followed, to see how hard it was going to be to get back to the car.

As I looked behind me, there, in a little oak that I had just passed, and that now was not more than twenty feet from me, I made out the round silhouette of a cock quail sitting motionless near the outer foliage. It flashed through my mind that it was the one bird that I should see within range of my gun this day. But how was I to obtain it? On the steep and brush-tangled hillside, I dared not attempt to turn quickly, for fear of injuring further my badly crippled leg. If I attempted to turn slowly, I was assured by the attitude of the quail that he would jump through the foliage and go out on the other side at my first move toward him. Standing on my one good leg, and steadying myself as best I could with the other, I cautiously turned my body as far around to the left as possible, held my gun in my right hand as one holds a long barreled revolver, and, in this strained position, attempted to shoot off the cock's head. In one sense it was the most sporting shot that I ever attempted. But luck was with me on this day, for I seemed to sway just as I pulled the trigger, and this proved to be what the situation demanded. At the shot the body of the quail fell out of the tree with the top of the head and bill entirely shot away.

I felt that this was a good shot. But the best shot that I ever saw made under difficult conditions in quail hunting fell to the lot of a man, who, in my boyhood, taught me to hunt. At the very beginning of the day, this man started through a barbed wire fence to get into the brush that lay above the dirt road along which we had come. As an experienced hunter always does in such a situation, he broke his gun and laid it over the third wire. Putting his weight on this, he started through the relatively wide hole thus made between the strands. Unluckily, the barbs of the wire strand next above caught in his shirt back and held him fast. At this moment, a small covey of quail, of whose presence in the neighborhood he was until this moment totally ignorant, flushed from the brush in front of him and made off up the hill. For a moment my mentor, with one leg on either side of the fence and with his shirt entangled in the wire above, held his position and did nothing but swear in extreme exasperation. Then, with his body still horizontal with the ground and, disregarding the wire that at once came up and fastened to the crotch of his pants, he somehow managed to get his gun together, to aim hastily at the last bird of the rise, and to fire. Perhaps he was lucky; perhaps he was unusually quick and skillful. At any rate, he killed his bird. I know of no successful shot at quail made under more difficult circumstances than this one.

The ability of the Valley Quail to carry shot is well known, yet even the experienced hunter fails to recover an occasional bird that he has killed because he did not see the bird flinch at the discharge of his gun. I will give two illustrations of this shot-carrying ability from my own experiences. The first happened one day when my hunting companion, John, and I were working uphill, one on either side of a willow-filled barranca. At one point in our progress, two birds jumped from my side and flashed over the tops of the willows. I shot at the cock, and I thought I had scored a clean miss, for the bird did not falter or flinch in the slightest degree. This miss did not bother me particularly because it had been a quick snap at a difficult target, and I continued on along the barranca edge. John, however, had heard me fire and had seen the cock as soon as it appeared above the willows. Yet, before he could bring his gun onto the bird, it fell dead to the ground just in front of him. I did not know that I had killed this bird until it was handed to me sometime later in the day when John and I came together again.

On another occasion a bird jumped from a large oak tree in such a manner that it gave me a quick snap shot at it. I fired, but the bird went on out of sight without flinching or faltering. Two hours later I chanced to be going in the general direction it had taken and in the center of a little trail I picked up my dead bird. I was a good hundred yards from the tree out of which it had jumped.

To the sportsman accustomed to using dogs when quail hunting, such sport as I have described will seem very strange. No doubt, he will wonder why more dogs are not used in this fine sport. There are several reasons. One is that the nature of the country is such that it is not suitable for hunting with dogs, for, in the excessively dry brush of almost any autumn, a dog working through it tires quickly and soon becomes useless. Another adverse factor lies in the birds themselves, for the Valley Quail cannot be relied upon to hold their place in front of a dog; they are more likely to move off steadily, somewhat after the manner of pheasants. Still another factor of undoubted importance, though one that is seldom considered, is that the use of dogs in the hunting field is a definite refinement of the sport; it becomes common practice only after the rough and ready shooting, such as I have attempted to describe, has passed. Now, as in the past, dogs are used occasionally by the quail hunters of the West, but the number of dogs so used never has been large in comparison with the number of hunters. As more and more land becomes fenced and closed to the public, it is probable that the number of hunting dogs in California will increase.

There are two features of Valley Quail hunting that the careful hunter soon learns to take into consideration. One consideration has to do with the last few bushes at the edge of any cover hunted. Ordinarily, as a hunter goes through a quail-filled patch of sage or other brush, the flushing birds become less numerous until they peter out completely as the edge of that particular patch is approached. The hunter, noticing this and taking it for granted that there is no use in going farther in that particular direction, may turn back before he comes to the last bush. To do this, oftentimes, is to miss the opportunity for a good shot or two; for the quail, moving forward with the hunter's progress, sometimes will come to the edge of the brush and there will hesitate, unwilling to face the flight over open ground until the last possible moment. This trait tends to hold one or two, and sometimes even more birds, in the very last bush or bushes, cover so slight that it would be scorned by quail at other times. It is always worth while to hunt the cover to the very last bush before turning back to retrace one's steps. It is perhaps this fear of open ground which causes the flushed quail to collect sometimes in the bushiest parts of little draws, rather than in the more open brush of the ridge faces.

A second consideration is the making of a good quail call which is a simple matter to the initiated. Any small piece of wood two or three inches long and a half inch square, and a wide elastic band will serve admirably. The wood is split with the grain, and a shallow slot is cut with a pocket knife in the middle of each half. The rubber band then is inserted lengthwise between the two halves, and one end of the call is tied tightly with string or another elastic band. By blowing through the slot a musical note is produced, and by stretching the elastic band at the unbound end this note can be raised in pitch until the proper sound is reached. A relatively low note is used to imitate the call of the cock quail, and a higher one for the hen. Usually, such a quail call can be counted on to stimulate a bird or two of a near-by flock to answer at least once or twice, and so it is sometimes of great assistance to the hunter in locating the flocks. Occasionally the possession of such a call will save the hunter many a weary mile of tramping.

In my younger days, I used to be able to call quail passably well simply by placing my upper front teeth against my lower lip and then calling through them, just as a boy plays a tune on a comb covered with tissue paper. With the passing of the years, however, my voice has deepened steadily, and so I can no longer do this simple trick successfully. I remember one day long ago, however, when I was more successful in this method of quail calling than I had any wish to be. At the time I was out with a companion in some high and very steep hills of the upper Santa Ynez Valley. While my companion chose to hunt along one side of a canyon near the bottom, I worked my way to the top of the high hills on the other side. It was a long, stiff climb, so when I reached the summit of the ridge I sat down on a boulder to rest. Then, having eased the pain in my calves—and recovered my breath, I began to call through my teeth as enticingly as I could. I remember that to my own ear I sounded pretty much like a quail. Presently a cock answered me from a hilltop far across the canyon. For three or four minutes we exchanged greetings pleasantly. After this the calling bird or birds became silent and, though I called repeatedly, I was able to elicit no further response. Presently I heard a commotion in the brush below me, and this grew steadily louder as I listened. Soon I beheld my companion, puffing and blowing from his hurried climb up the steep hillside, coming toward me as fast as his aching leg muscles could propel him. Seeing me at last as I sat quietly on my rock, he stopped short and in as eager a voice as his overtaxed lungs would allow, he asked me where the flock was. It was evident, I was astonished now to discover, that he supposed that there was a good covey of quail close to me on that hilltop. Suddenly I realized that he had mistaken my calling for that of a quail. This struck me as very funny, especially when I saw by his breathless, sweaty condition at how rapid a pace he had climbed the hill. I told him that there were no birds near at hand, and at this his face fell perceptibly.

"But I heard them calling from right here," he expostulated. "What happened to them, anyway?"

Laughing, I told him that it was I who had done the calling. However, he saw nothing funny in this bit of information. Instead, he looked at me in some anger and remarked that, at my age, I should know better than to play a trick like that on him.

Later, after a rest, he regained his good nature, and together we set out for the covey that I had located on the hilltop across the canyon from us. When at last we arrived on this second hilltop, it was interesting to me to find the birds several hundred yards closer to my former stand than they had been when they first answered my calls. From this fact I took it that, although the birds had ceased to answer me, they had kept moving steadily in my direction until we came upon them.

4

THE DESERT QUAIL

Lophortyx gambeli

The Desert Quail, known also as the Gambel's Quail, is the dandy of the family. One may not say positively that it is the handsomest of the quails, because hunters of other species, loyal to their own native birds, hardly will agree with such a sweeping statement. Yet its brilliant color pattern and its alert and jaunty bearing certainly make it the darling of every eye that beholds it. This bird's red-brown flanks are rich enough to fix one's attention on it at once, and yet they are not so brilliant as to be garish. They set off to great advantage its grayish back and black breast spot and topknot in a land where dull grays and parched greens are almost the only hues to be seen.

That the bird is a close relative of the Valley Quail can be seen at a single glance. Indeed, so closely does it resemble the latter bird in general color pattern, habits, and voice that many an incurious or uninstructed person, thinking the two to be of one species, does not take the trouble to mark the many minor differences between them.

I remember very well an occasion when I called the attention of a lady, who, as a tourist, was casually interested in any sight that the country had to offer, to a small flock of these desert birds as they crossed the dirt road on which we were traveling. Having reached the edge of the low-growing, open brush at the roadside, the covey paused for a moment and gave us an excellent, near view of themselves. The tourist looked at them intently for a moment and then, in a disappointed voice, she remarked that they looked to her just like the birds at home, that is, in southern California. This incident occurred on the Papagos Indian Reservation not far from San Xavier Mission in Arizona. This lack of perception on the lady's part astonished me somewhat. Since that time I have discovered that many quail hunters do not know the differences between the two birds, and so I have been forced to modify my uncomplimentary opinion of the tourist.

To the seeing eye, to the hunter who studies and who knows thoroughly the birds that he hunts, the two can hardly be confused. The breast of the Desert Quail is without the scaling that is so noticeable a part of the Valley Quail's markings. It is very light in color, and in the middle, when the male alone is considered, there is a large more or less circular patch or spot of black that is deep in the center and fades out into the light areas that surround it, much as a ball of smoke floating on the still air disintegrates about the edges. More than this, the forehead is black and not dirty white, and the crown and flanks are a rich red-brown.

The notes of the two birds are essentially different, as one discovers if he takes the trouble to listen to each one carefully. To my ear, those of the Desert Quail are more metallic. The alarm note is a series of "clinks" that might very well emanate from some machine made of tempered steel. The location call has a fourth syllable added to it: – "Cha quá qua qua." This extra syllable is very noticeable when the birds are calling. And there are many other differences of a minor nature.

Compared with the Bobwhite, the Desert Quail is almost mute, for it seldom twitters or peeps or talks as it moves about undisturbed under the scanty desert brush. This and other peculiar characteristics were clearly demonstrated to me one noonday in March as I watched a small covey on the high desert of western Arizona. The birds of this particular covey were very tame and trusting, and they allowed me to watch them at close range as they gleaned between the cactus plants and other desert forms that grew relatively thickly at this place. They showed no fear of me whatever so long as I sat quietly in my car, and I was able to observe that they moved along the edge of the dirt road without audible sounds. One hen had lost her tail in some previous misadventure; but as she ran erratically over the sand, I could not see that she was any the worse for this accident. Doubtless, she found it difficult to steer herself during those brief moments when she was on the wing, but I had no opportunity to confirm this belief by actual observation.

Wishing to see what would be the birds' reactions to me on foot, since they seemed to ignore me as long as I stayed in the car, I opened the door on the far side from them as cautiously as possible and inched myself to the ground. As my foot touched the roadway, the quail were off through the brush, running at so swift a rate that I lost sight of them at once. By fast walking I managed in about a hundred yards to overtake the laggards. These few birds rose at about forty yards and flew off into a near-by, dense clump of desert plants. At this point, and for the first time in the incident, they became somewhat noisy. I never saw the other members of the covey again.

The habitat of the Desert Quail is vastly different from much of that of the Valley Quail, and this difference unquestionably has led to many minor differences in habit. For one thing, these birds run more and faster. Their running ability is remarkable and quite beyond the belief of anyone who has not witnessed it. It is difficult, if not impossible, for the hunter to keep up with them. Unless there is much pot shooting, every bird the hunter brings to bag, after the first two or three, is earned by hard work in a hot and difficult country.

This skill in running does not endear the bird to those wing shots who not only will not shoot at birds on the ground but who are accustomed to birds that lie well to dogs. Such men are further exasperated by the shortness of the flights that the birds often make when at last they are put into the air. If the hunter is very quick with his gun, however, such flying birds do not present particularly difficult targets. Usually the flight is straight away, and the height attained seldom is more than ten feet. This makes for easy shooting. The cover, too, is usually open, and it is not too difficult to find the dead birds.

Considering these peculiarities of color pattern, voice, and habit, it is clear that this bird deserves to be classed as a separate and distinct species. In general, however, the Desert Quail and the Valley Quail are so much alike that anything that is said or written of the one is likely to apply almost equally to the other.

The range of the Desert Quail is fairly extensive, lying as it does on both sides of the Mexican Border and extending in an east-west direction from Palm Springs to El Paso. As far as my experience goes, however, I have found this quail much more abundant west of the Arizona-New Mexico line than east of it. In many places this range coincides with those of the cholla and the giant cacti and the road runner. Both the cholla cactus and the road runner have had an influence on the bird's economy, and so, too, has the mesquite, for the quail eat great quantities of mesquite seeds. But the giant cactus, or suhuaro, though an extraordinary and picturesque denizen of certain areas of the quail's range, seems to have had little or no influence on the bird's life.

The cholla, from the human point of view, is an amazing plant. To the hunter used to the uplands of the Atlantic and the Pacific coasts, it is a devilish floral development that makes hunting all but impossible in those wide areas where it flourishes. Possessed of the sharpest and strongest spines or needles, this plant commonly grows to ankle height, and stout is the leather that it will not penetrate. Often it grows higher than this, even to a height of four or five feet and, at a distance, takes on the appearance of a shrub. These larger specimens, however, give the hunter little trouble, for they are easily seen and, therefore, easily avoided.

My first encounter with the cholla remains vividly in my mind even after many years. I was hunting quail on the northern slope of a mountain at the extreme western edge of the cholla's range. At the outset of the hunt I had noticed an occasional spiny plant growing here and there on the ground, but all of them were small and looked harmless. Most were partially or wholly hidden by the coarse grass that grew upon the mountainside. Being more or less familiar with cacti in general from years of quail and deer hunting in southern California, I was confident of my ability to cope with this new variety, and paid little attention to the low-growing plants.

During this hunt I wore the light yet serviceable boots that, up to this time, I had considered ample protection against the spears of cacti and yuccas and all other thorns and spines to be found on an ordinary, arid hillside. This confidence in the stoutness of my boots was soon rudely shaken, however, for, at one point as I pressed upward in pursuit of a small covey of quail, my left shoe lightly brushed against one of these devilish cholla plants. The contact seemed very light indeed; yet spines entered the leather of the instep, and one spine went entirely through and into my foot. As far as my foot was concerned, no great damage had been done. When I started to remove the lump of cactus that now clung to the outside of my boot, I found myself involved in a struggle not unlike that famous one between Hercules and the Hydra.

The lump of cholla divided into smaller and still smaller lumps each time that I tried to remove it, and these smaller lumps fell here and there and attached themselves determinedly to whatever they happened to fall upon. Then these smaller parts subdivided again each time that pressure was exerted to remove them. It was a most exasperating and time-consuming performance; my temper was not improved by the knowledge that all the while that I struggled with the cactus, the quail that I was following were on the move away from me and up and across the mountainside. After this experience my shooting was ruined for the day, because I did not dare take my eyes from the ground as I pressed forward through the grass and low brush. No one can hunt pleasantly or successfully under conditions of this sort; and, of course, the quail that I followed got away. At last I gave it up and went home in disgust.

The road runner, a large form of the cuckoo, has taken to living on the ground and on a diet of animal forms that are found there. It has a bad reputation both by inheritance and by acquisition. This long-tailed, heavy-billed bird is an expert lizard catcher; yet it does not confine itself wholly to these reptiles. It will eat even the large, long, and coarse-haired black caterpillar, a creature usually avoided by other searchers after food because of the menace of the sharp, heavy hairs. Though it incubates its own eggs, many a farmer accuses it of eating other birds' eggs, hens' eggs in particular, and he shoots it on sight.

My friend Kearney Moore, gamekeeper, with headquarters at Aguila, Arizona, has seen the omnivorous cuckoo kill and eat baby Desert Quail. On one occasion he saw a road runner gobble up nine chicks out of a single brood without interference from the mother quail. This is surprising because the quail is known to be a fighter. A cock Valley Quail, for example, will so torment a cock ring-neck pheasant, if confined in the same cage with the latter, that the pheasant will spend the whole day on a perch as high above the ground as the top of the cage will permit. A pheasant is as large as or larger than a road runner, yet in these encounters with the latter, witnessed by Kearney Moore, the mother quail made no efforts to defend their young.

Fortunately for the Desert Quail, the road runner does not exist in large numbers. It brings off from three to five young each year, and these juvenile birds, keeping to the ground as they must do, are easily caught by all the furtive creatures of the coverts who prey on animal life. By these means the road runner population is kept down, and the quail does not suffer as much as it might otherwise.

The roosting habits of these Desert Quail are not essentially different from those of the Valley Quail. They, too, roost in trees wherever possible, selecting the densest foliage that can be found. Along watercourses there is no lack of suitable trees and tall shrubs, and in certain parts of the open desert there is sufficient precipitation to nourish such vegetation as mesquite and ironwood. It is true that the latter is not a very dense-foliaged tree, yet the quail do use it for roosts. In other parts of the desert, however, there are few plants that reach the magnitude of trees, and here the quail must get along as best they can on what is available. It is generally believed that the quail's chief enemies in these sections, particularly in the quarter light of early morning and late evening, are the cats, the coyotes and similar animals. If this is true, a good, stout shrub will serve the quail as a roosting place almost as well as will a tall tree.

My only first-hand information on this important point, obtained in the field as I have gone over the desert in search of quails, is that the large, mammal-hunting hawks have greatly outnumbered all other species of Raptores seen there, save only the little sparrow hawk, which does not prey on quails. Of owls, the small, mammal-feeding species are greatly in the majority. Though I have found these Desert Quails almost uniformly in or near the desert brush, sparse-growing and scraggly as it may have been, I definitely have the impression that they were not expecting attacks from the air when so situated. This observation further strengthens my opinion that the Desert Quail has most to fear from attacks on the ground, the place where it spends so much of its time.

Like all our other quails, this desert species is extremely regular in its movements. This trait was illustrated very clearly to me one noonday when I asked a game warden in western Arizona if there were any coveys near at hand to which he could take me at this time of day.

"Certainly," was his ready reply, "there is a small flock near an old road about three miles from here."

Driving to the spot he had indicated, the warden looked about and remarked that the birds should be there. In less than two minutes we saw the birds. To the hunter, looking for birds on the almost limitless face of the desert, this trait is one to be remembered always.

It is generally taken for granted among western hunters that any topknotted quail seen east of the San Jacinto Mountains can safely be assumed to be a Desert Quail, and that any such bird seen to the west of these mountains surely is a Valley Quail. As a general rule, this one does very well, even though there are places where it does not hold. At Palm Springs, for example, there are to be found both Desert Quail and Valley Quail, for the ranges of the two species overlap here. This area is a very favorable one for the quail hunter. So far as I have observed, few if any of the residents attempt to distinguish between the two kinds of quail. Both are simply "quail" to them and are hunted impartially and in the same way. In the mountains back of the town there are also a few Mountain Quail, and so here, within a few miles of this small center, can be found all three members of the group sometimes referred to as the "California Quails." It is probable that there occurs here some small amount of interbreeding among the topknotted species and, much more rarely, there

may be an occasional misalliance between a plumed Mountain Quail and a topknotted Valley Quail. If this latter interbreeding does indeed take place, it must be a very rare occurrence. The only basis for mentioning it is that I have seen one skin that seemed to be that of a bird sprung from both sources.

One early spring day at Palm Springs I had a very amusing and instructive experience. Inquiring at a gasoline station for information about the local quail populations, I was told that there was a very large flock of "painted" birds on a certain date ranch. When I inquired about the actual size of this flock, I was told that it must be a very large one because "the other day" enough quail had been taken from it to meet the needs of a quail dinner for twenty-five people. This indicated a very large flock indeed. Inasmuch as the open hunting season had passed long since, and the bag limit was fifteen birds, the hunter who was reported to have killed all these birds certainly must have disregarded the game law. This latter phase of the report, however, was of only academic interest to me at the moment.

"Were there any birds left in the flock after this slaughter?" I asked my informant.

"Plenty more!" was the instant reply.

I drove out to the famous date ranch and, having located the proprietor, asked if I might look over the quail on his premises. This request met with a very cold reception. Perhaps he thought that I was a game warden checking up on his hunting activities. At last, after much argument, the proprietor gave me the necessary permission and directed me to a place on the ranch where, he said, he thought I was most likely to find the birds. Following these directions, I did my best to locate the covey. Even though I brought to bear every bit of quail lore I knew, I could not find a single feather nor did I hear a single bird call. There were many quail tracks in the loose sand about the salt bushes and other tangles at the edge of the orchard. I even saw a rabbit or two, but at the moment, at least, there was not a single quail to be seen or heard.

At last I came on a laborer who was irrigating the date trees. Explaining my mission to this man, I received the most sympathetic hearing and help. He told me that the quail spent the mornings along the eastern edge of the orchard where I was at that moment, and that about noon they moved some three hundred yards to the western line of the farm, roosting at night in a line of tall tamarisk trees that grew there. As it was then four-thirty in the afternoon, I went to the place indicated by my new friend, and, on hearing them twittering amiably to one another, I found the covey in the heart of a great salt bush.

I had hoped for a good look at these birds, but at first sight of me, a small flock of perhaps fifteen ran together and then flushed straight into the setting sun. All that I saw of them was the black forms hurtling through the air.

These birds, as is the custom of the Desert Quail, flew less than a hundred yards and then settled on the desert floor. In this desolate place the greasewood bushes grew far apart, making it easy for me to see the birds as they stood motionless at the bases of these shrubs in singles and pairs. As long as I stood motionless where I was, there was little movement among the frightened and wary birds. As soon as I moved a single step toward them, they set off at a swift run for other and more remote bushes. Yet, even as they ran, individual birds here and there would stop for a brief instant to pick up some particle of food that they found in their path. This trait was surprising to me. It seemed to indicate that these were thrifty souls, unwilling to leave any little tidbit of food ungarnered, even though they so obviously thought they were running for their lives. Here, undoubtedly, was a trait of character acquired from long residence in an arid, and, therefore, a partially foodless land.

Several other characteristics common to the individuals of this species of quail were demonstrated in this episode. The limited range of the covey was especially well shown, for this particular date farm was hardly more than twenty acres. There was little or no evidence to show that the birds ever left it during the months of flock life for expeditions into the waterless waste land surrounding the farm. The regularity of movement of the birds, also, was particularly noticeable.

As to the number of individuals in this flock before it was shot up, I was able to arrive at no satisfactory conclusion. It was evident at once that a flock of but forty birds would not yield the twenty-five necessary for the quail dinner unless traps, rather than guns, had been used in the capture. It was possible that a large portion of the original covey had moved to other ground after the shooting, though this seemed to me to be unlikely because I could find but two expended cartridges on the sandy ground. These two empty shells did not indicate a terrifying barrage. It was possible that I had come on only a small portion of the flock, the other and much larger part being elsewhere at the moment of my arrival. Weighing all these uncertainties, I could come to no final conclusion that completely satisfied me. I left the date ranch but little wiser in regard to the particular point that had taken me there.

About half a century ago, before the automobile and the concrete highway, it was a common occurrence to see flocks of Desert Quail, some of them very large, in the brush close to the dirt road as one drove slowly across the desert. This condition is largely changed now.

On a trip of about three thousand miles that I made in June, 1947, I saw not more than a score of birds from my car. There are several reasons for this. One is that the modern motor car commonly travels at such high rates of speed over these straight, improved pavements that the eye cannot pick up small motionless objects in the near-by brush, even though it be the widely scattered, stunted bushes that make up the desert brush. Another reason is that quail no longer frequent the roadside as they once did. In these days of motorized sports, many a hunter considers it sufficient sport merely to sit in the front seat of his automobile with a shotgun or rifle at his side, and to drive until game is discovered. Then he jumps from his car and takes a shot or two quickly; he may even shoot from the seat of the car. This unfair and unlawful practice has been very destructive to the game of all sorts that formerly fed along and across the highways of travel, and the remnants of the flocks and herds thus attacked now have retreated far back from the roads.

There is still one highway of travel, however, along which the Desert Quail feed with little molestation from man, and from which hurried glimpses of them can be had by interested travelers. This is the railroad. It is true that the noise of the rushing trains often frightens these coveys into hurried rises from the screening brush in which they have been feeding, and so for the most part one sees the birds when they are in the air. Yet there are times when a covey, even one relatively close to the track, will not take fright and flush when the train passes it. When this happens, a keen eye at the window will get a brief glimpse of the birds on the ground.

In one September afternoon's travel from Douglas eastward toward El Paso I saw from a Southern Pacific Railroad window at least a dozen of these desert coveys. The coveys that I saw rise to the passing train averaged, I estimated, thirty or more birds apiece. Of those that remained quietly on the ground, I was able to make out only four or five birds before the speeding train carried me past them. The coveys were spaced fairly regularly, at about ten or fifteen minute intervals. Along this way there were very few evidences of surface water, and so I took it that the quail managed to get along without drinking water for relatively long periods of time.

A covey of thirty Desert Quail seems to me to be about the sized flock that a hunter can reasonably expect to find on the desert today. Formerly there were flocks very much larger than this in favorable locations. Even today large flocks are sometimes encountered, but these are the exception rather than the rule. The number of men who hunt the Desert Quail is steadily increasing. Now that the Valley Quail is not as available to the shooter as it once was, many a sportsman who lives within striking distance of the desert is turning his attention that way. Los Angeles, for example, with its population of more than a million, is turning more and more toward the east for its quail shooting. As the number of hunters increases, and as the killing power of their guns increases, the size and the number of the coveys of the Desert Quail become smaller and smaller.

One day in early summer when another quail hunter and I were driving across the desert in Arizona, something about the appearance of Texas Canyon caught our eyes, and we stopped to look over the place a little more carefully. As we moved cautiously across one of the sandy floors between two ridges of huge sandstone boulders, a female Desert Quail suddenly moved out onto the open sand from the base of a thin-foliaged shrub. For a moment or two she watched us as we stood there motionless. Then she moved well away from the shelter of the bush and walked nervously yet slowly across the bare sand. Occasionally, as she moved along she bobbed or nodded her head far forward three or four times in a very peculiar manner. When at last she came to another bush, she stopped there for a moment. Then she went on in the same uncertain way to a third bush. At this we went forward to the place where we had seen her first, and here we discovered a cluster of tiny chicks not much more than a day or two old. I do not know how many there were because we made no effort to count them. Perhaps there were as many as fifteen. At first they stood motionless and stared at us. Then, as we approached a step closer, they went running, almost flowing, in a tight bunch over the stems of the shrub at the base of which their mother had left them. Having no wish to scatter them, we stepped hastily backward at this show of frightened motion and made a wide circle around the bush. No doubt the mother returned to them as soon as we were hidden from her view. As an incident in the life of a quail hunter, this was not a very great one, yet it was pleasant out of all proportion to its importance and something I shall always remember.

One point raised by this chance meeting, that of the likelihood of this quail family getting water to drink regularly, is of considerable interest. So far as I could tell from a brief search made there, no spring or other source of surface water was in the immediate neighborhood. It appeared that these quail could get along without water for a considerable time.

Another quail family that I saw about this time, a cock and a hen without chicks, also made a deep impression on me. I had spent the night on the sand in a dry camp at the mouth of a sandy wash in the mountains immediately south of the Santa Catalinas. Very early the next morning I was moving up the wash slowly and cautiously in the hope of coming on Desert Quail. In this place, as in Texas Canyon, there were no outward signs of surface water. Moving around a great boulder, I discovered the two birds on the open sand. They saw me, as was to be expected, and, though not greatly frightened, they began to move away from me. The cock agilely ran up to the top of another large boulder and for a moment or two stood there and inspected me with an alert eye. In the clear, early-morning light the rich red-brown of the flank took on a particularly lively hue, and the black face, surmounted by the jaunty jet-black topknot, contrasted splendidly with the pale lemon breast. At that moment I judged this individual to be the handsomest quail that I had ever seen, and time has not altered that judgment.

5

THE MOUNTAIN QUAIL

Oreortyx picta

The Mountain Quail is at once a symbol and a challenge, for, in most parts of its range it dwells high in the rugged mountains; and the hunter or bird lover who would come upon it in its native surroundings usually must be willing to expend considerable time and energy in the search for it. Most often, I suppose, this bird is encountered by deer hunters in summer and early fall as they scour the upper hills for their furtive quarry, and by hikers and campers as they scramble over the rough shoulders and the brush-covered canyon sides of the sierras. Occasionally a fisherman, as he stands knee deep in the waters of some cold, rushing, mountain stream, or as he travels up and down the stream bank, sees a bird or two for a moment as they forage across some tiny clearing not far from the water. The Mountain Quail has come to symbolize, in most minds acquainted with it, all that is fine, free and exhilarating in life at the higher altitudes. To those who never visit the heights, the Mountain Quail is but an unfamiliar name.

This quail ranges over the mountains of the entire state of California, as well as over parts of Oregon, Washington and Nevada. There are definite reports of Mountain Quail even in western Arizona, though this is somewhat out of their generally accepted range. I have encountered them in such widely separated areas, to mention only three of many, as the western slope of the Coast Range near Santa Barbara, the eastern slope of the Sierra Nevadas back of Independence, and the Williamette Valley of southern Oregon. Three more distinct and widely differing climates than these would be difficult to find in the West; yet the Mountain Quail is at home in all of them.

No accurate computation of quail populations in extensive rough country can be made, of course. It is, however, a recognized fact that the lowland bird outnumbers the highland one by a very considerable margin.

A Valley Quail flock of a hundred birds is no very great covey even today, while a Mountain Quail flock of twenty birds is only rarely seen. There are probably many times as many flocks of the former as there are of the latter. Occasionally one hears of very large assemblages of the big, straight-plumed species, but so far as the individual sportsman is concerned, these large coveys remain a matter of hearsay and are almost never personally encountered.

In southern California the birds keep to the tops of the mountains, for the most part, all through the spring, summer and fall, and they are not often found below an altitude of three thousand feet. This is about the upper limit of the range of the Valley Quail, and here the two may sometimes be found in the same locality, as on Figueroa Mountain in the Santa Ynez Valley, though not in mixed flocks. In late fall, when the first cold weather sets in, both species move to lower levels, the Mountain Quail going down into the upper levels of the summer range of the Valley Quail, and the Valley Quail dropping still lower near the canyon bottoms. William Leon Dawson, in his book entitled "Birds of California," gives the range of the mountain bird as lying between two and eight thousand feet.

The Coast Ranges immediately back of my home, where a few small coveys of these birds live, are formed of strata that rise at a sharp angle from the ocean to an altitude of almost four thousand feet in the first range, and to six thousand in the second. Between these two lies the Santa Ynez Valley, the home of large coveys of Valley Quail, but an impassable barrier to the Mountain Quail except to the eastward, where the two ranges come together. The axes of these ranges are east and west. The southern face of the first, or coast, range is formed by layers of sandstone, but the top of this range and its northern slope, where the sandstone largely has been eroded, are composed of shale. In this shale, with an occasional outcropping of sandstone, are to be found scattered clumps of big-cone pines and, in the deep creases, colonies of Douglas fir.

All these trees, however, are more or less incidental, for the primary covering of the whole range is a blanket of almost impenetrable chaparral: scrub oak, Ceanothus, toyon, sumac, cherry, bay, and many others of similar kind. In the summertime, water is to be found only at great intervals, and then never in abundance. One might almost say that for at least three or four months of every year this area is without surface water for the great bulk of its smaller inhabitants with limited means of travel. The Valley Quail, for the most part, avoid this region, preferring the more open and sage-covered areas, and they usually enter the chaparral only when frightened from their home ranges. The Mountain Quail, on the other hand, find this a congenial habitat and spend their entire lives here. It is essentially different cover from the sage, and the Mountain Quail, living in it, have acquired bodies and habits different from those of the lowland quail.

In the first place, the Mountain Quail seldom flies above the brush, even when frightened. If you come on this bird suddenly, it may rise with a great explosive whirring of wings, and rocket off above the chaparral for twenty or thirty yards, but much more often it will make away on its stout legs under the brush and, therefore, out of sight and reach of the hunter. For this reason, most sportsmen find the Mountain Quail but indifferent sport and few of them take the trouble to pursue it except when they want a quail or two to sweeten the camp pot.

Usually a traveler in the chaparral districts, whether a hunter carrying a gun or a bird lover with binoculars, first becomes aware of the birds' proximity when he hears them running over the dry twigs and leaves, and he then catches a glimpse of them only by lying prone on the ground and peering under the canopy of brush that is all but impenetrable to the eye a yard above the shale. Many a time I have become aware of the nearness of these quail by hearing them as they made off under the brush, and have succeeded in catching fleeting glimpses of them, if I managed to see them at all, only by flattening myself on the ground.

One of these occasions I remember with particular clearness, because on this day I had gone into the chaparral with the express purpose of finding a covey of Mountain Quail, and, against every reasonable chance, I had been successful. All through the fall it lay in my mind that many months earlier I had seen a small flock of the big, red-flanked birds in the mountains some three or four miles back from my home. On this particular day, when the need for a bird or two of this species had become pressing, I had set out on foot with a .410 single shot shotgun in my hand, to look for them where I had previously stumbled upon them. I climbed slowly up the steep, chaparral-covered mountains, and at probably a little over fifteen hundred feet, I heard what I thought was a quail moving off under the Ceanothus close beside me. The correct interpreting of sounds in the dry leaves of the chaparral calls for nice distinctions: the rattlesnake makes a continuous, scratchy noise as it moves off; the towhee scratches often and energetically, with a perceptible pause between each scratch, as it turns over the leaves; the thrasher flicks the leaves sideways two or three times with its bill before it pauses to search for food; and the quail patter off lightly, yet steadily, as they run or walk five or ten feet and come to a halt to see whether they are being followed.

On this particular occasion, hearing something moving under the brush, I stood and listened to determine what creature it was that disturbed the dry leaves. For a moment all was quiet, and then there came to my ears once more the steady rustle that could only be made by quail. At this I lay down very quietly, and searched the stems in front of my face for a sight of a straight plume or a dark red-brown flank. At first I saw nothing but stems. Then a slight movement about twenty feet from me betrayed the bird's presence. Taking as careful aim as was possible under the circumstances, I fired and killed the bird, as I had hoped to do, by a shot or two on the outside of the charge's pattern, and without tearing my quail. At the shot there was a great rustling of the leaves, but I caught glimpses of only a bird or two, and these but for the briefest moments.

I reloaded and waited, and soon another bird, close to me, moved just a little and disclosed only a part of its body to me. This time my shooting was less skillful, or the shot bunched on the discharge, which is unlikely, for I tore the front part of the bird's head entirely away and thus ruined it for exhibition purposes. Again I waited, hoping against hope that I would see another quail, but from then on I saw no more. Soon they were clucking and calling in the thick brush in front of me not more than thirty-five or forty yards away, but I could not get sight of them. In a little while they had moved off over the curve of the hill, and I had lost them for that day.

I kept the untorn specimen for several days, exhibiting it frequently to my shooting companions. It was a very handsome bird with its long, straight plume, the rich red flanks, the black under-tail coverts, and the gray-blue breast.

In other and better-watered altitudes and latitudes than ours, the Mountain Quail is not bound so closely to any single source of water, even though the individual coveys may prefer to drink at the same place day after day, as they do hereabouts. In the Sierra Nevada, where innumerable rivulets, streams and lakes are to be found scattered throughout the range, and where showers may occur at any time, the birds may be encountered almost anywhere in areas that are suitable for them. Though heavily timbered, there is much brush also on these mountains; chinquapin, a low-growing, dense tree, is particularly in evidence in many places, and there is much other, similar cover. The coveys roam about under this dense foliage, appearing for a moment here or there in some tiny clearing, or as they forage at the brush line. Occasionally a flock is encountered on the granite under the tall conifers, and when this occurs, a good view of the birds can be had. Farther north they are found at lower levels, but in these rain-drenched lands, the foliage, though of a different type from that of the Sierras and of southern California, is no less dense and impenetrable to the human eye. And so in that locality as well, the birds are only seldom seen for satisfactorily long periods.

In appearance the Mountain Quail is a striking bird. Some hold that it is the most beautiful of all the quails. It is noticeably larger than the Valley Quail, and its topknot consists of two long, narrow, straight feathers, usually held together as one, but sometimes divided and carried as two that radiate from the same base. These feathers are held, for the most part, erect on the head. Like the plume on the shako of a West Point cadet, that of the Mountain Quail gives a strikingly handsome and alert appearance. Down each flank is a broad, red-brown patch of the richest shade and barred or scaled heavily with white. The throat pattern, though not as distinct as that of the Valley Quail, is similar to it, the black being replaced by a rich red-brown. The breast is slate blue, and the under-tail coverts are black. The male and female are identical in color pattern, however, which is a distinct variation from the usual scheme of things among the quails, and one followed by only the Mountain and the Scaled Quails in the United States.

The ordinary note of the Mountain Quail, when heard at a little distance, is a low-pitched call of one syllable, not very different in timbre from the double note of the poor-will, or the musical hoot of the pigmy owl—if one can call this pleasantly soft note a hoot. When heard close at hand, a second low note is audible. Once having heard this call, it is not difficult for a hunter or hiker to imitate it so successfully that he will receive many an answer from birds hidden away in the brush. The quail give this particular call at intervals of a minute or more as the birds, sometimes alone, but far more often in coveys of from six to eighteen, roam over the mountainside.

One day in the early summer, as I was fishing in the Truckee River, I paused in midstream to watch a bird that I took to be an unmated male, as he wandered under the pines over the rough and steep canyon side. This bird wandered about in a restless, aimless way. As he wandered, occasionally he would pause, stretch out his neck to its limit, and give this rather pleasing whistle. Though I watched this single bird for some time, I did not see any others in that vicinity, and I concluded that, even as late in the season as it was (July), this bird still was mildly hopeful of finding a mate.

These quail have another note, a sort of cluck, very hard to keep in mind, yet unmistakable whenever heard. It is not very unlike the cluck of an ordinary hen, though by no means as loud. This they use constantly when they are in coveys, a low, running, conversational series of notes that can be compared in character to the much lower cluckings and twitterings of the Bobwhite in similar situations.

They have still another common note or series of notes, that is heard most often in the mating season and that is beyond translation into words. To my ear, which admittedly is rather dull in distinguishing between sounds of a closely similar nature, it is a weird booming that rises in volume to a peak and then gradually dies out. On the swelling slope of the mountainside, this throbbing cluck resounds strangely, almost mysteriously, over the quiet, peaceful landscape. In a narrow, high-walled canyon, where at times sunlight and shadow pattern the creek bottom and the piled boulders so gloomily, it is almost eerie.

In late May, I went with a companion to spend two or three days on the north slope of Figueroa Mountain, a peak in the San Raphaels, or second coast range. There had been late rains this year, very late indeed for this section which seldom has any rainfall to speak of after the first week in April. We found the mountain still brilliant with all the life and color of spring. The creeks were full, and wild flowers were growing everywhere; godetia in particular was in evidence in great showy patches. The mountain sides, usually at this time of year beginning to dry out, were seeping water in every gully and cut bank. As we topped the ridge and started to drop down into Fir Canyon, we heard a pair of Mountain Quail call from the timber above us. Then, as we descended, we heard others calling from both sides of the deep canyon. Still farther downstream, a pair ran from a little pool in the canyon bottom up the steep hillside and disappeared behind a big, sprawling rock maple. We made camp that evening close beside the creek in the canyon bottom on the only level land large enough to hold our blankets. As we cooked our supper over an open fire, we heard the Mountain Quail calling first here and then there, on every side of us. It was a memorable occasion.

There were many other birds to be seen in the woods on this particular jaunt, and we found many nests. One California Jay in a thick lilac bush sat so close that we finally poked her from her nest with the tip of a fishing rod. We even found a junco's nest not more than a hundred feet from our blankets. To me the junco is the trimmest of all that trim family which comprises the sparrows and the finches. It is a northerner and a mountaineer whom I always regard with unfeigned enthusiasm. The female is a demure bird of quiet gray. This particular female junco's nest was in a cup-shaped hole or depression on the face of a four-foot cut bank. Grasses growing just above curved gracefully down over the nest, shielding it from the outside world, and here the bird sat without movement and patiently waited. Those three days and nights of fishing and hiking and sleeping high up on the mountainside were made many times more delightful for us because of the junco and the jay, and because of the quail, both seen and unseen, whose pleasant calls came floating down to us through the still, fragrant air.

Anyone unacquainted with the habits of quail in general, doubtless would have thought that there were very many Mountain Quail in the woods around us on this occasion. But I am sure that such was not the case. It was spring, and, therefore, the small flock that lived in that area was now split up into perhaps a dozen pairs. These pairs in turn were scattered widely as they sought out suitable sites for their nests.

Sometimes, the birds are found in small, outlying clumps of scattered brush, and on these occasions it is possible for the hunter to have a few minutes of fast shooting. Even in these situations, when all the dead birds are retrieved, usually it will be found that the bag is not a heavy one. I had an opportunity of this sort one fall day when I was hunting well up on the side of Figueroa Mountain. My companion that day knew of a flock of quail that lived in an isolated patch of manzanita and other brush that grew in a tiny, steep canyon. We found the birds just where he said they would be in the draw at a particularly steep part of the mountainside. It was a small flock, perhaps fifteen birds in all, and so, under any circumstances there was little possibility of prolonged sport. At the first encounter, a bird or two rose on the wing and offered fair shots, but the others ran off on foot. I noted the spot where one of these latter birds hid at the foot of a scraggly manzanita bush. When I walked toward its hiding place, it remained on the ground motionless, though in half sight, until I was close upon it. In my experience no Valley Quail has done this in a similar, exposed situation. It flushed at last with a great noise of wings, and drove at tremendous speed straight down the mountainside. As this was a straightaway shot, even though a fast one, I managed to make it successfully, and the bird fell dead far below me. My companion, down the mountainside from me, was not presented with such straightaway targets as this, for other birds that I put up passed him at right angles with all the force of gravity, as well as that of their powerful wings, propelling them downward. Yet, even on such difficult targets, I saw him make two successive kills cleanly. Doubtless, he was an excellent shot. From this covey we took four birds before the others disappeared from before us.

Aside from the shooting, it was interesting to watch these hurtling birds come to ground when traveling at such tremendous speed. As they were loath to leave the small patch of open bush in which we had found them and in which they evidently had been living for months, probably all spring and summer, the flushed birds flew but a little way down the mountainside and then came to earth. They did this by swinging sharply to the right or left in a tight half circle, and then banking heavily up the steep mountainside with all wing and tail feathers set as widely as possible. This skillfully executed turn and bank brought them to a standstill in a surprisingly short space and with seemingly little difficulty.

What enemies this hardy mountaineer has to face and outwit can easily be guessed. I suppose that the wildcat is as deadly to this bird as is any other mammal. There is another, however, neither mammal nor bird, against which the quails in general, and this quail in particular, seem to be defenseless. This is the forest fire. Late in the summer, when the chaparral becomes very dry and from one cause or another takes fire, there comes a desperate time for the quail, the rabbits, the rats, mice and chipmunks, and all the other wild creatures who survive in ordinary times because of their ability to hide in the thick brush. Once a fire is started, the wind is likely to carry it over and across the mountains in an irresistible wall of smoke and flame. The heat is intense, and every living thing in its path is consumed. Usually in the mornings during such a conflagration, there is little or no wind, and then the fire burns slowly, with the tendency to die out along much of its front. At these times the quail can keep moving out and away from its path. About noon, however, a wind may spring up and fan the smoldering embers to flames once more, and when this happens the whole line is quickened to new life and energy. Unless the pace of the fire is too fast, even now the deer, coyotes and the other larger mammals can be counted on to move out of the country before the flames reach them; and so, too, do many of the birds. But the quail, the rabbits and the squirrels, creatures who all their lives have found the thick brush of the locality a haven of refuge in every other time of danger, now move into the deepest and thickest brush, and there await the fire that is to destroy them.

When a fire is sweeping the mountain range, it does not travel at a uniform pace. It may burn for hours in one place and hardly advance at all. Then it may reach a favorable slope and bound up it with all the speed and fury of an immense, ravening wild beast. The heat at such a time is unbelievably great. If the wind and the lay of the land are right, a whole mountainside will burst into flames almost in an instant, while the fire that is the source of the heat is still a half mile away. When this happens, animal life on that mountainside is utterly destroyed. I have heard firefighters tell of bands of quail that they have seen dive into the thick clumps of brush in the very path of the onrushing fire and cower there until the flames reached them and they were consumed.

For weeks after such a forest fire, the burned area lies denuded and bare of life. At first glance it would seem that it must remain this way for many years, but luckily this does not happen. The plants of the region have developed the remarkable ability to stump-sprout from the charred remnants of their stems, which now thrust up starkly an inch or two above the dirt. Within six weeks after the fire, little new shoots are to be seen, and within the year, if the rains are good that winter, these little shoots will have grown to stems two or more feet long. Then come the deer, for they like best to browse on these new and tender growths, and they are sufficiently strong travelers to find new pastures. In time the quail and the other more sedentary forms of animal life move in from the surrounding areas that were not devastated. Usually within seven years, the chaparral is again so thick that it is difficult for a man to force his way through it and, unless the fire has covered too large an area, life goes on about as it did before. With luck, it will be twenty or even thirty years before another fire burns over this region, and the quail have ample time to renew themselves there.

One morning, when I was hunting Valley Quail in the sage a little below the chaparral belt with a friend who had just come from Connecticut, we had an amusing experience with a little covey of Mountain Quail. For reasons that were not clear to me, we were having no success in locating Valley Quail, and I suggested that we climb higher and try our luck on a covey of the big, straight-plumed species that I had seen once or twice in other years in the high but fairly open brush under the Digger pines at a certain place in Davy Brown Canyon.

Ardent hunter and good shot that my friend was, ordinarily he would have jumped at such a plan. Now he held back. Soon it became evident that he, never having heard of the existence of the mountain bird, was inclined to believe that this was a hoax of some kind.

I convinced him, at least partially, of my sincerity, and he agreed to go with me. As we went up the mountainside in our automobile, I explained at some length the peculiar habits of the quail we were going after. Particularly did I impress on him the necessity for fast shooting if and when a quail was put into the air.

"These are ground-loving birds under thick brush. The best chance a man has to get one or two of them into the air is to fire at one on the ground as soon as he sees it. If this is done, one or two others near by may be frightened enough to be flushed. Once up, however, they will fly only a little way and will fly very fast. You will have to be quick with your second barrel if you are to drop a second bird."

Crossing the ridge, we began to drop down the rough dirt road into the canyon. I turned off the engine and coasted slowly and all but noiselessly. When we came opposite the spot that I had in mind, I heard a quail cluck once or twice.

"Here they are," I said. "Walk straight up to them. Kill one bird on the ground and then be ready for whatever happens."

Following these directions, he walked cautiously forward while I took up a position a little to one side. Almost at once he saw a quail in a little path between two bushes and he fired at it. Then he fired again, his second shot following the first so quickly that the two almost blended. At this I heard other quail rise through the tall brush. One went past me at about ten feet with all the speed and noise of an express train. For all its speed and noise, however, it offered me the easiest of targets, for it flew straight away from me at about head height.

"How did you come out?" I called to my friend.

"Oh, all right," he answered in a disgusted tone. "I shot one bird on the ground, as you told me to do. Then a towhee came up right over it. I was trying so hard to be quick with my second barrel that I killed the thing before I saw what it was. When the three quail came up, my gun was empty!"

I told him then, quite truthfully, that his second shot was as fast and accurate a one as I had ever seen made, but this praise did little to comfort him.

One morning in midsummer, while camped on the shores of Lake Tahoe near Emerald Bay, I hid myself in some low-growing bushes under a big yellow pine in the hope that by so doing I might catch a glimpse of a deer, a porcupine, or perhaps some bird common in that region, but unknown to the shores of southern California. I was almost completely covered, yet I had so arranged myself that I had a fairly full view of the area immediately in front of me. Since this particular morning was warm and balmy, not such weather as was likely to stimulate the wild folk to energy and movement, it did not seem likely that I should witness any major display. One never knows, however, when Nature will reveal her treasures; and so, having comfortably seated myself with my back against a yellow pine, I waited pleasantly for whatever form of life might present itself.

For some time nothing stirred in the little world that I could see. The sun shone warm, and the magnificent conifers moved their feathery limbs slowly and gracefully in the intermittent breeze that came in from the blue lake. At last I noticed some motion under a chinquapin. Then out into the clearing there ran a baby Mountain Quail hardly a week out of the shell. In a moment another followed the first, and then another and another appeared, until there were perhaps a dozen and a half in the tiny clearing before me. They were traveling, roughly, in a semicircle, if it could be said that they kept any formation at all. Immediately behind them, forming the focus or center of the arc, came one of the parents. Finally, about twenty feet behind this center, came the second adult bird.

The little chicks ran hither and yon over the coarse sand of the clearing, eagerly searching for choice morsels of food. The alert mother, for I take it for granted that it was she, moved slowly and daintily forward just behind the chicks, keeping careful watch on every side for any possible sign of danger. The bird in the rear, I regret to say, seemed to me merely following along behind his numerous family, and he was not being a very helpful part of it.

When they arrived in the center of the clearing, where the sunlight seemed to me to strike the warmest, I half expected each member of the family to pause in its travels long enough for a dust bath, but in this I was disappointed. Perhaps the sand was too coarse for their taste, perhaps the joy and excitement of being alive was too great in each little breast to allow them to stay so long in any one place. Whatever it was, the chicks scurried here, there and everywhere, while the mother bird stood as erect as possible on her two sturdy legs and searched the brush around her with unwinking scrutiny. I counted the chicks time after time with varying results; one time I counted ten, and a moment later I counted twenty-one. I found it impossible to arrive at the same number by any two consecutive

counts, and so I took a rough average of them all, settling on the number seventeen as most likely correct.

At last, at a distance of some thirty feet, the mother bird caught sight of me, and froze. I froze also, not allowing so much as my eyes to move. This action on my part seemed to confuse her somewhat. For a little while she seemed to be uncertain about me, whether I were indeed an enemy, or something inanimate, and she studied me first with one eye and then with the other. In this dilemma, she at last flew to the top of a four-foot stump not twenty feet from my hiding place, and for some moments from this point of vantage she stared at me intently. During this unwinking scrutiny I continued to hold myself as motionless as possible, and by so doing, in some measure allayed her first suspicions. But she did not feel sure enough of me to keep her chicks in my immediate neighborhood, evidently, for she now jumped down from the stump and, with every show of concern, led her family off into the chinquapins on my right. The last I saw of them was a glimpse of the back of the male as he ran after his already departed family. For some time after this I waited, hoping against hope that the family would return. When it became evident that they would not come back—that the show was over, with some reluctance, I arose and went back into camp.

The next time I saw a Mountain Quail, after this particularly pleasing and intimate glimpse of a whole family, was in a restaurant on the Auburn-Sacramento Highway. A mounted skin, covered with dust and cobwebs, stood on a little shelf on the wall for the delectation of the patrons of the place. As I looked up at the unhappy effigy, and compared it with my mental picture of this bird as I had seen it in the woods about Lake Tahoe it came over me with force that here is one creature, at least, that does not lend itself gracefully to the taxidermist's art. Since then I have examined with care every mount that I have come upon and I have found every one to be unsatisfactory.

Pictures, too, aside from actual photographs by skilled artists, fail to give even an approximately correct impression of this fine and handsome quail. One, a color plate by Fuertes, which shows the bird on a flat rock in the act of giving its mating call, does carry the mind up to high mountain country, but the bird is so obviously misshapen and out of proportion that one finds little pleasure even here. The reason for all this is, I think, that in all these representations there is lost, of necessity, that quality of elusiveness that is one of the bird's most attractive characteristics.

In the mountains one sees it for a moment only, a mere flash, it seems, so many times, and then in a definite and close background or setting. Sometimes one sees it partially hidden at the base of a Ceanothus bush, sometimes poised for an instant on a rock as it looks back quickly at its pursuer, and then it is gone. In a picture it stands starkly open to the public gaze, and there is no cover for it anywhere. Kept captive in the usual flat, bare, dirt-bottomed cage, it is almost equally out of place, and only the nodding plumes give any suggestion of the beauty and vivacity that are its birthright.

One day in early September I was walking under the pines and through the scattered brush a half mile back from Lake Tahoe, when I heard what I took to be two or three quail running away from me. I stopped at once, and immediately three half-grown Mountain Quail burst out of the bushes and made off on the wing. Then another and another flushed, until seventeen had showed themselves. In the middle of this display, both parents jumped into a young fir rather close to me and watched the flight of their brood with obvious agitation. Dr. Joseph Grinnell, author of "The Game Birds of California," gives the nesting season as lasting from April to the middle of August. My own more limited experience with the birds indicates that they nest much later in the Tahoe region than they do in our Santa Barbara mountains, and that broods of young birds may be seen there well into September.

One day in early January, I set off over the snow on the floor of Yosemite Valley to see what birds were abroad. It was cold, so cold that men went about muffled to the ears, and every breath condensed as they exhaled. Although it did not seem to be a favorable time in which to find many of the feathered folk, I felt that any glimpse vouchsafed, however small, would be of unusual interest—and so it proved to be. Soon I saw a bird or two of unknown species moving in the young trees and brush at the side of a tiny draw, so I bent my steps that way. The birds that I first noticed turned out to be jays and one or two others; and then, suddenly and quite unexpectedly, I made out a Mountain Quail.

This bird evidently had seen me before I had seen it, and so I had but the briefest glimpse of it on the ground. As soon as I stopped for a better look, the bird flushed and went off at rocket speed into a tangle of trees and shrubs a hundred yards away. Two others that I had not seen on the ground went out after this one, and this proved to be the whole number of quail there. One cannot but wonder if that was all that survived of the family that, in early summer, probably numbered fifteen. On further inspection, I found that the birds had been on the bank of the draw down which, for a few feet, there trickled a tiny stream of warm water from the Ahwahne Hotel. Undoubtedly this was the warmest spot on the valley floor that cold day. Every year since, I have returned to this spot at this time and have searched for these quail, but I have not been able to locate them again.

A friend of mine had an unusual experience with Mountain Quail that is altogether different from any of mine. He and two other men found a flock of perhaps five hundred birds in low sage not far from Winnemucca in Nevada. These birds in this cover acted very much as would Valley Quail in the same situation, and all three men had a splendid shoot. Each man killed his limit that day, making a bag of seventy-five birds. I have never seen anything comparable to this episode, either as to numbers or habits.

Farmers in Mountain Quail country almost invariably speak of the tameness of these birds when not hunted or otherwise persecuted. This reputation is borne out by game breeders who have handled the birds. This endearing quality of the Mountain Quail is in marked contrast to that of the Valley and Desert quails, which are wild and hard to handle to a degree. Indeed, the gentleness of the big bird in captivity is one of its most appealing characteristics. One would suppose that this would have a definite bearing on its egg-laying and nesting habits when confined, making it one of the most prolific of layers, but this supposition does not prove to be true. It is difficult indeed to induce the birds to lay. This failure to lay while in a cage is the chief reason for the relatively high prices demanded for quail of this species by game breeders—three times that of the Bobwhites, and four times that of the Desert Quail.

6

THE MASSENA QUAIL

Cyrtonyx montezumae

Of all our quails, the Mearns's Quail, perhaps, is the most interesting. Certainly this bird is the one of which the least is known. The textbooks tell us that it is the northernmost form of the Massena or Montezuma Quail, just as the Bobwhite of New England is the northernmost form of *Colinus virginianus;* that the range of the species extends far south into Mexico; and that the name of this particular subspecies is *Cyrtonyx montezumae mearnsi,* a difficult mouthful for the average untutored tongue to pronounce. It is found, if indeed the searcher is lucky enough to find it anywhere in the United States, along the Mexican Border in Arizona, New Mexico, and Texas, as well as in Mexico. How far south into Mexico it extends before it merges with the Mexican form of the species can only be conjectured.

Searching the records for mention of this little known bird, one finds much to excite his curiosity and to stimulate him to further search, but he finds little factual knowledge to satisfy him, other than the skins that are to be seen in almost any of the larger museums, and a too brief paragraph here and there in a bird book or magazine of ornithology. For example, soldiers who marched with General Taylor in 1846 saw this ground-loving bird scuttling across their path as they campaigned about the Mexican city of Monterrey. Although preoccupied with the pressing affairs of war, these blue-clad men noticed and commented on its peculiar habits and markings. Undoubtedly Geronimo, the Apache, knew it well, for he was at home in its favorite coverts; but he, unfortunately, did not see fit to leave us an account of its life history. Cattlemen saw it in the rocky ravines of Arizona and New Mexico as they rode after their herds in that arid and mountainous country. These men called it the Fool Quail because, when frightened, it sat so close that it could be approached and, sometimes, killed with a stick. Fuertes, the famous illustrator of bird books, spent some months in its native haunts in search of it and other species common to the Sonoran Zones, but he saw only a very few Mearns's Quail. Of those quail that he did see, he was able to collect one cock only, and that on the last day of his stay. Henshaw, on the other hand, saw and took many specimens in a later year. One comprehensive series of volumes on birds of the United States, recently published, is of the opinion that the species now may be extinct north of the border. Several other competent searchers, who have gone into Massena Quail territory both north and south of the Line, have declared this quail to be one of the most difficult to locate and to take, even after its low, owl-like call has been heard at fairly close range.

So the short record goes. When one comes to the end of it and closes the last book, it is with a consciousness that the picture is far from complete. Yet it must be admitted, and in spite of the incompleteness of the record, that a bird capable of inspiring comments of this nature can hardly fail to be interesting when actually found.

There are three approaches to such a rare creature. The first and easiest is through the museums, where skins can be seen and studied, and where carefully prepared books and pamphlets may be read. The second is the game farms, where a few live birds can be thoroughly and intimately studied as they carry on their lives in cages and pens. The Mearns's Quail is a rare bird even here, however, and is not to be found on every game farm. At first thought, this approach appears to be rather unsatisfactory, yet there is much to be learned here. Some important information can be discovered at the game farm that can be found in no other place. The third and most satisfactory approach is in the dry, rough, and hot mountains of our southern border. Here, by the exercise of much ingenuity and an almost infinite patience, a few glimpses of the bird in its native surroundings may be hoped for. While these glimpses may in the end prove to have been all too brief, they are sure to have been interesting and instructive. If all three approaches have been followed, and their respective results brought together, it may be that a readable, though far from complete, story will be the result.

As one compares the skin of the cock Massena Quail with that of another American quail—the Bobwhite or the Valley Quail—the most striking feature of the former, aside from the bizarre color pattern, is the exceptionally heavy legs and feet. It might be said that they are twice the weight of the Bobwhite's feet. And herein seems to be the key to the bird's character. Of a family of ground birds, this member is the one best fitted for a life spent wholly on the ground. Every field record to be found and every glimpse of the live bird bears out this observation. Fuertes, for example, was unable to secure a specimen before the last day of his stay in Massena Quail country largely because he could not induce the birds, which he succeeded in flushing only after much effort and many attempts, to fly more than a rod or two. In that short interval he was unable to get his gun to his shoulder and on the target, and he was given no opportunity to shoot a bird on the ground.

Swarth succeeded in observing a limited number of Mearns's Quail, and he records that in one location he found them scratching out tubers a full two inches under the surface of the soil. It should be observed in passing that it takes heavy legs and feet and much strength in a quail to dig two inches into the untilled soil. The tubers sought by the birds in this manner are known as "nutgrass," and are one of the bird's chief articles of diet.

As might be expected, with the heavy legs goes a heavy bill, to assist in the arduous work of excavation. Fuertes has illustrated these structural peculiarities in his sketches of the bird, but they are likely to pass unnoticed unless definite attention is called to them.

This quail is generally considered the smallest of all the American quails. Its length is given in the bird books as being about nine inches. However, this is not absolutely accurate. If one goes wholly by this measurement of nine inches, it seems that the Massena Quail is not more than three quarters the size of the Mountain Quail, whose length is given as twelve inches. If one watches the Massena Quail as they go about their business in the stony ravines near Fort Huachuca or under the pines of the higher White Mountains, the impression of smallness is very definite. Yet there is more to the comparison than this. The feathers of the Mountain Quail, for one thing, are very long and broad, and this gives the bird an appearance of size that is not borne out completely when the plucked body is placed beside that of the Valley Quail, its nearest relative geographically and a bird commonly held to be noticeably smaller in size.

The reverse illusion holds in regard to the Massena Quail, whose feathers are relatively short and narrow, and whose tail is so short and weak as to give the impression of being almost useless as a rudder when the bird is in flight. Indeed, so short is this tail, reaching, as it does, only just beyond the under-tail coverts, that it adds definitely to the bizarre appearance which has come to be the outstanding characteristic of the species. It is the shortness of the tail, I believe, as much as anything else that causes some observers to liken this little quail to the much larger and but distantly related guinea hen of the farmyard. Certainly it is smaller than the Valley Quail, the Mountain Quail, or the Bobwhite, but it is not actually as much smaller as it is said or as it appears to be.

The markings of the cock Mearns's Quail are unusual for an American quail. Each man who studies these markings seems to find different relationships from those attributed to the bird by other men. Granted at once that the color pattern is a superficial basis for comparison, it is a fact that it is a most interesting and commonly used one. The head and throat pattern of this bird does bear at least some resemblance to the same markings of both the Common and the Masked Bobwhite when the three are considered together; and, therefore, it is with the color pattern of the Bobwhite that, for the most part, I shall compare the markings of the Mearns's Quail.

The head and throat pattern of the Mearns's Quail cock is a series of sharply contrasting brown, black, and white lines that give to the bird an almost artificial and clownish appearance. One is tempted to say, when first seeing these lines in a picture, that nature does not color her children that way. Yet one can imagine, I think, that the more simple pattern of the Bobwhite may have been broken up by some chance mutation into this highly complicated one. At any rate, if one closes his eyes to the lines within the more usual head pattern of the cock quail, the throat shield and the strongly marked superorbital line can clearly be distinguished. The red-brown band of the central belly of the Mearns's Quail might suggest the lighter red-brown of the breast and belly of the Masked Bobwhite and of the red phase of the eastern Bobwhite, just as the bluish gray breast suggests the similar marking on the Mountain, the Valley, and the Desert quails.

All likeness to other quails vanishes, however, when the crest is considered. Here the Mearns's Quail is peculiar. The long feathers of the crown curve down over the back of the head and can be spread sideways at will by their owner.

The back pattern is shot through with tiny lance heads of cream or light buff and, therefore, is somewhat like the back pattern of the Masked Bobwhite. These lance heads seem to be a part of the regular color pattern of the back but, on the Mearns's Quail, on close inspection it is discovered that they are merely the light colored shafts of the dark feathers and are most strongly in evidence when the feathers become much worn. They give the back as a whole a peculiar, broken appearance, which fits in remarkably with the cover in which the bird is usually found. This was proved to me very forcefully on one occasion when I tried to approach a Mearns's Quail so carefully that I would be able to see it on the ground before it flushed. Everything seemed to favor such an attempt. I knew where the quail was squatting. The grass at that spot was short and very thin, and the light was good. I could not have asked for a better opportunity. Yet I failed completely to discover the crouching body. I did not see the bird until, at last, it rose and flew off. It is interesting to remember that there are similar lance heads or spikes, though usually less conspicuous ones, on the backs of all young quails in juvenal plumage, as well as on those of most of the grouse.

The white dots or spots on the gray of the breast and flanks are of considerable interest because they are somewhat unusual and because in the juvenal plumage they are black and not white. There are similar, though larger, white spots on the flanks of the Elegant, or Yaqui Quail, white on red-brown in this case. The under-tail coverts are black, as they are in the Mountain Quail.

When one looks at the back and tail of the Mearns's Quail, however, all close likenesses to any other American quail vanish. The tail is so short and weak that it seems impossible that its wearer is closely related to any of our long- and strong-tailed native quails. Viewed from the rear, the Montezuma Quail has an obvious and striking resemblance to certain of the more or less common quails of northern Africa—to the quail of the Bible, *Coturnix coturnix,* for example. This superficial resemblance to species so far removed from it geographically adds another item of interest to *Cyrtonyx montezumae mearnsi.* In a family of strong flyers, the hawks, for example, such a resemblance would not be startling. As a matter of fact, sparrow hawks are reasonably much the same the world over. That such a localized and weak-flying bird as the Mearns's Quail should resemble even slightly a quail in Africa is exceedingly strange.

I had my first glimpse of this quail in real life one September day in 1939, and under very unusual circumstances. I had sat all the long and hot afternoon at my window in a Pullman car on the Southern Pacific Railroad, and from this questionable point of vantage had watched for glimpses, brief but interesting, of the Desert Quail and other forms that inhabited this region through which I was traveling. It was a hot and arid land, sparsely grown to the usual desert shrubs and weeds, one that at first glance promised no glimpse of wildlife whatever. Yet, in the course of the afternoon, I had seen many flocks of quail, at average intervals of perhaps fifteen minutes. These intervals spaced the coveys at about ten miles.

Here and there a jack rabbit had gone scurrying off at an acute angle with the tracks and never straight away. Once I saw a fine red coyote who was so unconcerned with the passing train that he never gave it a glance.

Some time after we left Bisbee, Arizona, however, we came to a more elevated region. The usual, somewhat monotonous desert growths gave way to grass. This change in flora suggested a possible change in avifauna, especially since the area lay so near the Mexican Border. More than usually alert now, I kept watch from my window. Soon this concentration was rewarded beyond anything for which I had hoped. As the train went thundering eastward over a rather extensive plain, a pair of small quail flushed from the thick grass not more than twenty-five or thirty yards from the track, and at about the same distance ahead of my window. By the greatest good fortune, I was looking at that moment at the general area from which the quail sprang, and I saw them as soon as they appeared above the grass. Both birds were, naturally, somewhat flustered by the noise of the train, and came buzzing out of the grass much like bumblebees. The hen made off straight away from the tracks in a normal though hurried flight and came to earth after perhaps forty yards. The cock, apparently much more befuddled than his mate, rose almost straight up on rapidly whirring wings to a height of about forty feet, performing somewhat like a bird that has been shot in the head. Then he passed over the train and through the smoke cloud in a frantic curve that carried him out of my sight. How far he flew after this before grounding I did not see. This introduction to the Mearns's Quail, brief as it was, was so unusual as to make it highly satisfactory. It is not likely that I shall have a second and similar encounter with these rare birds even though I travel many times over this same route.

As this experience amply demonstrates, the Mearns's Quail is a creature of the grasses in elevated lands. Many a time, perhaps, it may be encountered in bushy thickets; yet every hunter and rancher along our southern border, who knows the birds at all well, will tell you that this bird bursts from a tuft of grass immediately underfoot as a man searches the hills for deer, or goes riding on horseback quietly up the canyons. In such cover, the unusual pattern of its back helps greatly to conceal the bird. Generally, mammals, birds and fishes have dark backs and light bellies. The theory is that such coloration makes the creature possessing it somewhat difficult to see both from above and below. This general color scheme is not followed by the Mearns's Quail. It has the expected dark and neutral colored back, it is true, but the under parts are even more darkly and conspicuously colored. It seems apparent that the Mearns's Quail can afford to sport any color on its belly that chance or natural law gives it because, being a grass-loving bird, there are few enemies with eyes set sufficiently low to see this area.

One February day, a little before noon, I went with two others up a little dry canyon situated not many miles north of Nogales, Arizona, to look for a little covey of Mearns's Quail that for some days past had been seen there with more or less regularity. Coming to the place where they most frequently had been observed, we scattered and searched the dry, grass-covered hills and the canyon floor for an hour or more for a sight of them. On this day we neither saw nor heard a single quail. Knowing the sedentary habits of the species, we were confident that they were just out of sight in some hidden nook or cranny that we had failed to locate. A movement, a call, or even a tiny patch of color in the grass almost surely must have betrayed them to one or the other of us. Yet we failed to find them that afternoon, and eventually we came in from the search empty-handed. This is a good example of how difficult it is to come on the birds by systematic search; yet I have the strong feeling that, had my companions, men who were at least partially familiar with the birds in that particular canyon, paid just a little closer attention to the exact whereabouts of the covey each time that they had seen it, as well as to the time of day, we could have walked almost directly to it.

The year 1938 seemed to be a particularly favorable one for these birds, if numbers are a true index of good and bad years, in all the region of southern Arizona. Wherever I went in Mearns's Quail country during this season I heard tales of their abundance. Yet just a little way north of these areas, the natives seemed to be entirely ignorant of the existence of the species. To these people the term "quail" infallibly meant the Desert Quail, which species also was abundant at this time all over its western and southern range. In and about Fort Huachuca and in the mountains to the southeast of Tucson it was relatively easy to get accurate information on the localities where flocks of Mearns's Quail could be found and studied. At least three coveys were to be found about the Fort itself.

This quail seems to be particularly vulnerable to the cold of a severe winter, just as the Scaled Quail suffers most and may be all but exterminated by the droughts of summer. The Mearns's Quail is a mountain loving species, with an altitudinal range of from four to nine thousand feet. In the low, arid areas between these altitudes it is not found. This range, not essentially different from that of the Mountain Quail on the Pacific Coast, as far as altitude is concerned, but totally different from it in cover, may become very wintry indeed during a cold year. This cold weather may last well into what, in other parts of the Southwest, is called spring. For example, in April I have driven in an automobile from Williams to the Grand Canyon in a snow storm so heavy that it threatened to make machine travel impracticable while the storm lasted. During periods of really severe cold, the Mearns's Quail suffers greatly, and at these times it often dies out over relatively large areas.

At the present moment it is the settled policy of Arizona to refuse collector licenses to all those who wish to take specimens of the state's avifauna. There is much to be said in favor of this policy, for in many areas the collectors have run wild, working destruction, in the name of science, that hardly can be justified. The state, impelled by the same motives, I suppose, also refuses permits to the game farmers to take and keep Mearns's Quail within Arizona. This seems to me to be a mistake. A carefully worked out plan here might build up a large stock of these interesting birds on the game farms with but trifling cost to the state. Once this was accomplished, those areas where the Mearns's Quail population has suffered disaster could be restocked as soon as the weather moderated, and the perpetuation of the species within the United States would be assured. The greatest obstacle, however, to the propagation of the Mearns's Quail on farms seems to be its unwillingness to lay, except under the most favorable conditions. It is a species that seldom is seen in aviaries, and its price during ordinary times is set at about seven times that of the Valley Quail. During some years, a single bird may be valued as high as $50. In the spring of 1947 I was offered two cocks for $35, but, before I could find a hen, these two were sold to someone else.

In the spring of 1934, while I was at the North Hollywood Game Farm studying and photographing the Benson or Yaqui Quail imported from Mexico, I heard that there was a pair of Mearns's Quail to be seen at the state game farm to the east of Los Angeles, so I went there to look at the birds. I saw them, but what a discouraging exhibit they turned out to be! Because of the danger of sickness, which is the greatest difficulty that breeders of game birds have to combat, this pair was penned in a wooden box about six feet wide and perhaps twelve feet long. The bottom of their cage was of small-mesh wire raised some six inches above the ground. One end of the box was open to the sunlight for about a third of its length. A more unsatisfactory place in which to house wild birds, except for its obvious sanitary feature, I have never seen. The manager of the farm very kindly lifted a wooden door at the closed end of the cage and allowed me to look through this opening at the quietly standing birds. Of all the quail that I have seen, save only those that were mounted, these two heavy-footed Mearns's Quail, raised on wire above the soil that is so dear to them and refused any close shelter, were the most pitiful in appearance.

If this bird were known by the title of "The Mountain Quail of the Mexican Border," or some similar appellation, much confusion would be saved, for this title is exactly descriptive of the bird. Oftentimes, as in parts of Arizona, it is found on so rolling or almost flat a plateau that the actual altitude of the region is not brought sharply to the attention of the hunter or observer. The Mountain Quail of California, on the other hand, is called a mountain quail, and so it is known by all to be a bird of the upper altitudes, and no one thinks to look for it in the low country. Unfortunately, the Mearns's Quail is not properly named, and so this one of its most distinctive characteristics is not known generally. It is a mountain species, and it is usually found on mountains and plateaus at altitudes well above the four-thousand-foot level.

One afternoon a friend and I located some birds of this species in a side canyon in the southern Rockies of New Mexico, the Sacramentos, at an altitude of almost exactly eight thousand feet. Searching carefully through the timber, we found a hen that so obviously had a nest containing eggs that she was incubating within a few feet of the spot where we saw her first that we did not stay long in that immediate neighborhood. By the luckiest chance imaginable, we were shown another nest by Roy Goslin, a young lumberman, who was working in this side canyon and who had made his discovery quite by accident. Stimulated by all this good fortune, we spent the night in a little clearing in the pines near the head of the canyon and at first sign of dawn the next morning we were up and about. As was to be expected in such a place and at such a time, the bird chorus was magnificent, and to add to our pleasure, from a point in the forest immediately across the canyon from us came the sound of a bear tearing apart a rotten log. There were wild turkeys, too, in the region. On the previous afternoon we had seen a great hen with a family of fifteen or more little ones, but these birds now did not betray their presence to us by either sight or sound.

After listening to the chorus for a moment or two, we set out to search for quail in the pines just below us. Having been told by Mr. Wimsatt, the owner of the property, that the quail commonly "used" the fields near the edge of the forest, we confined our operations to this general area. Presently a cock called in the pines not far in front of us and at just a little higher level than we were at the moment. He was answered almost immediately by another cock, also in the pines, just across a little draw. For some time these two birds called very softly and very sweetly back and forth across the clearing that lay between them. It was a single note not unlike, in quality, the call of the poor-wills of our Coast Range.

After listening for a while to this conversation, we set out very cautiously and very quietly to find the callers. In this effort, however, we were completely unsuccessful. At the start, it seemed that we had located the callers almost exactly, but when we arrived at the spots where we had supposed the birds had called from, we found not the slightest trace of either of them. Giving it up at last as hopeless, we returned to the nest site near the top of the ridge and spent the next hour in photographing it.

The nest of the Mearns's Quail is of extraordinary interest. The one we photographed was carefully hidden in the long grass and weeds under a low-hanging pine branch. The nest itself was made of grass and was almost spherical in shape. The opening was toward the east, and through it we could see eight eggs. The hen had not completed the clutch, apparently, for at no time did we find her on the eggs. We did come on her once, however, as she seemed to be moving up to the nest to deposit another egg. Studying this nest carefully, we were reminded that we had been told at the game farm at Carlsbad that the Mearns's Quail in captivity there would lay only when nests were made for them that met their rather exacting requirements.

In my searchings for this rare bird I count myself to have been unusually fortunate, for I have seen it in many places and under many different conditions. The picture of it that has held most strongly in my mind is that of a cock that walked by me broadside one evening, on bare ground, so that I had a clear and unobstructed view of him. I saw clearly the stripes on the head and throat, the tiny dots on the flanks and side, and the little lance heads on the back. For the only time, I saw clearly the ends of the drumsticks as they appeared below the wing and flank. On these the feathering was black, which made the bird appear to have on short, black knee breeches.

I have talked with men who have shot this bird both in the United States and in Mexico, and I have read accounts written by others who have had similar experiences. One hunter near Benson spoke of having stumbled by chance on a covey of Mearns's Quail when he was looking for either Desert or Scaled Quail and of having had a good shoot even though at the time he had no idea what kind of quail it was that he was shooting. Considering the precarious hold on continued existence that this species has, the indifferent sport that they offer and the often great labor that is involved in finding even a small covey of them, most true sportsmen will hold it to be a matter of conscience not to disturb them when they are by chance come upon.

7

THE SCALED QUAIL

Callipepla squamata

The Scaled Quail has not been bountifully endowed with those bright colors that are the pride of most of the other members of the family. Only the female Valley Quail, which it resembles in so many obvious ways, is as plainly clad. To the man used to seeing the Bobwhite of the Atlantic Seaboard, or the Valley Quail of the Pacific Slope, or the Elegant Quail of western Mexico, this quail of our Southwest presents a very drab appearance indeed. Like the female Valley Quail, its sides and belly are heavily barred or scaled, a pattern that on this species continues across the breast and shoulders to the throat. The flank feathers, which fold over the closed wing, are almost identical in pattern with those of its western relative. Unlike the Valley Quail, this bird does not have a topknot. Its crest, though high, is not particularly noticeable at a little distance to an observer whom the quail is facing, because it is a neutral gray just like the rest of the head. The individual feathers of the crest, however, are peculiar in that their undersides are very light in color—almost white, in fact; and so, when they are raised, their white under sides become conspicuous to eyes behind the quail, and they give to their owner its common field name, "Cottontop." When flattened, as they are when the bird is foraging, the long feathers project to the rear at a sharp angle with the nape and appear to be a heavy barb. This crest, when held high, gives its wearer a wide-eyed, distinguished appearance. It is the bird's chief ornament.

The Scaled Quail's body, when compared with other members of the clan, is somewhat flattened and when viewed from the rear has an almost turtlish appearance. This is especially evident when birds of this species are seen in an aviary with other quails.

If nature has endowed this quail very scantily with color, it has been rich in its gifts in other respects, for although the bird lives in a habitat that would be the despair of all its American relatives, it not only holds its own there, but seems to be happy and contented. Only the Desert Quail dwells in a land approaching this one's range in aridity and in scantiness of cover. Drought, when in succession the dry years follow one another, is the bird's most constant companion and worst enemy, one that kills more individuals than all other foes combined. In 1903, 1904, and 1905, there was a sequence of disastrous droughts; and again in 1923, 1924, and 1925. These dry spells all but exterminated the quail over much of their range.

This question of the dependence of quails upon water is of such unusual interest that to be even partially understood it should be considered from a wider point of view than that of the birds alone. Certain mammals have learned to get along comfortably for long periods of time without drinking water. Among these, many of the rodents are conspicuous. The rats and mice of the desert obviously are able to live without drinking water, and even the common house mouse, I think, drinks little in many of its apartments. Among the birds, the hawks and the owls get their fluids from sources other than pools and streams. A sparrow hawk, which I kept in a small cage as a pet, lived for years without taking any water whatever, even though, during the first months of its captivity, I kept a dish full on the bottom of the cage.

Because we are so dependent upon water, we take it for granted that all other creatures are limited by the same dependence; and so there is much argument on this subject among hunters. It is the opinion of many experienced men, especially those who have shot western quails, that the birds go to water daily to drink, just as do the common hen and the well known mourning dove. On the other extreme are those who say that the desert species get along very well with no water at all. I have even heard it said, rashly, I thought, that if you give a Desert Quail a drink of water you will kill the bird.

My own opinion is that all of our quails like to be near water, that they are at their best when some permanent water is available. One has but to go along the shores of the Colorado River, for example, to see how closely some of the coveys of Desert Quail keep to it. On the other hand, it is equally clear that many coveys live contentedly without any water whatever for long periods of time. This last observation is especially true of many Scaled Quail living on both sides of the Mexican Border. Even the Scaled Quail, however, does enjoy a good drink on occasion. I have seen birds in a wild state drink with obvious satisfaction at times when the land was not in the grip of a terrifying drought. The same thing may be said with equal truth of the Desert Quail.

F. L. JAQUES

When the dry years come along, as they do all too often on the ranges of the Scaled Quail, the birds suffer greatly and many die. I believe, however, that the suffering, in many cases, is caused by the more or less complete drying out of the foods that the birds find at these times, and by the fact that the food becomes more and more difficult to find until at last it fails completely, rather than by the actual absence of drinking water. Desert, Valley, Mountain, and Bobwhite quails seem to be affected by droughts in about the same way as are the Scaled Quail, though it must be noted in this connection that the term "drought" is a relative one. The ranges of these different species, taken in the order given, become progressively more humid. Therefore, it is obvious that conditions that might be termed as those of a drought in the usually well-watered uplands of Carolina certainly would not be considered so by the Scaled Quail.

H. L. Stoddard, author of "The Bobwhite Quail," states that a Bobwhite may go as long as two weeks without drinking water during a particularly humid period of the year. Once I kept a pair of Masked Bobwhites from Sonora confined in a cage for observational purposes. I saw these birds drink only two or three times from the bowl of water with which I supplied them, and on each of these occasions the hen took only a sip or two. After I had filled the drinking fountain when it had been dry for perhaps twenty-four hours, I would rarely see the cock swallow several billfuls of wet sand from beside the basin. I did not see either bird drink as a hen would have done in the same situation, that is, take billfuls of water and, lifting and tilting back the head, let the satisfying fluid run down the gullet. In this connection it might be interesting to remember that the average person, when he goes out on the desert from a more humid climate, consumes twice as much water daily, usually a minimum of a full gallon, as he does when he is at home.

As a game bird the Scaled Quail is not as famous as some of the other members of the family. Hunters of the Ruffed Grouse and the Bobwhite in the East, and followers of the Valley Quail in the West almost invariably find this bird somewhat disappointing when they set out to hunt it in its own territory. This disappointment arises from a number of causes, I think, and not from any one. The nature of the country in which the bird lives certainly will be one of these, for, in addition to being an arid and a drought-afflicted land, it is likely to be covered with growths of one kind or another that are devilish in their ability to make passage through them a misery. There are, for example, the various cacti, the mesquite bushes, and the cat's-claw. Where this last-named plant flourishes, there is no pleasure to be had by either man or dog. One stand of cat's-claw in eastern Arizona I remember with particular repugnance because it stopped me completely at each point that I attempted to enter it. In this place the individual shrubs sent out from the root stems in every direction lithe, willowy branches from six to ten feet long. Each slender branch carried hundreds of needle-sharp thorns shaped almost exactly like cat claws and about equal to them in size and retentive power. When an arm or leg came in contact with the outermost twigs of a branch, the little thorns bit home in flesh or cloth, and the forward motion of the hunter caused the other claws on the brush end to make contact, too. It was as though the bush had reached out and seized the hunter by his arm or leg or body. In such a grip, there was no going forward. Each time that I was seized, I backed up slowly and disengaged myself as best I could. In the end, I gave up the quest as hopeless, even though I knew that there were many quail in this cover.

Another disappointment for the foreign hunter is that the Scaled Quail is extremely unwilling to rise from the ground and seek safety in flight. This bird is a runner of distinction, and it almost invariably trusts to its legs rather than to its wings when it is approached too closely. It runs steadily and so fast that not every hunter is able to keep up with it. Much of the shooting, of necessity, is on the ground, a fact that does not endear the bird to men who fancy themselves as wing shots. Frederic Remington considered the running ability of the Scaled Quail the outstanding characteristic of the bird. He stated, it seemed to me with some astonishment, that it requires more skill to hit it on the run than it does on the wing. Many another sportsman will agree with this, I think.

Although a particularly competent runner, the bird does take to the air on occasion. At such times it may not fly as far as the Valley Quail, but it does fly for short distances. A single individual that I came on unexpectedly one morning in the great Huachuca Wash, at an altitude of about forty-five hundred feet, flushed and flew off over the light brush for about twenty yards. Then it dropped to the ground and ran off at so fast a speed that I was unable to come up with it again. Two birds, one after the other, performed in a similar manner in the grass and weeds of a hillside not far from Santa Fé.

Because the bird is seen to fly so little, many hunters are confirmed in the opinion that the Scaled Quail is not a powerful flyer. This opinion is not justified by the facts. Within its own needs, the bird is an expert flyer. This realization came to me as something of a surprise, for, like so many others, I had theretofore considered the quail to be a ground bird, one that ran exceptionally well and seldom flew. To see it spring from the ground in a frightened rise to a height of four or five feet, check its speed and turn in a full half circle to avoid hindering obstructions, and return to the ground within ten feet of its starting point struck me as unusual. A mourning dove in the same situation would have required three times the space for the maneuver, or, being a creature of less steady nerves, it would have been unable to do it at all. I have seen Scaled Quail repeat this performance several times.

The difference in temperament between a dove and a quail is very noticeable. Of the two birds, the former is much more given to sudden, even senseless, panics. When a hawk appears on the scene, the dove seems to lose all sense except its frantic impulse for straight, fast flying. If confined in an aviary at the moment, it may kill itself against the wire. Undoubtedly, the dove's emotions are governed in this case by the fact that it is a bird of the open fields, and that it eludes its pursuers, if at all, by straight and swift flight. The quail, on the other hand, is a bird of the brush-covered hills, and it eludes its enemies by hiding in the densest cover. It is the quails rather than the doves that are most often attacked and taken by hawks. One might reasonably suppose that the quails would become more panicky when an accipiter hawk shows itself, yet this does not seem to be the case.

I had my first view of a Scaled Quail one morning in 1913 when I was in a little cabin on the high desert not far from Silver City, New Mexico. While still in bed, I heard from without a curious bird note, a sort of clucking, that lured me from my warm blankets. It was a cold morning in late fall, and I shivered as I stood at the open window and searched the limited area open to my vision for a sight of the caller. In a moment I saw a roundish, gray bird that sat perched on a little shrub about a foot from the ground and close under my window. Because of the cold, this individual was fluffed out to its fullest extent. Occasionally it gave the clucking note that had attracted my attention in the first place.

This commonplace experience illustrates very well the tameness of this species when not persecuted. Farmers and ranchers of the Southwest will tell you that it feeds commonly in the barnyard with the chickens on those ranches where no shooting is allowed. There it shows little or no concern over the relatively close approach of human beings. Confined in a cage, it becomes gentle and trusting. A pair that I had in my quail pen brought off a brood of nine young the first year that I had them. This in itself tells much of the steadiness of these birds. How tame the fledgelings would have become I was not destined to know, for they drowned themselves one after another in the little pool that is a part of my aviary.

The inability of baby quail to keep out of water seems to be widespread, and it extends even to so distant a relative as the Button Quail of the Philippine Islands. Even though I have seen adults of this species swim across my tiny pool rather than take the trouble to go around it or to fly over it, I have known of their tiny young drowning themselves almost en masse in a basin so small that no one would have thought such a feat possible.

The most often heard calls of this species are ones that might be compared to the "bobwhite" and the "whee oohhh" calls of the Bobwhite. The first, an "oh′-oh, oh′-oh, oh′-oh", uttered very much as a man might say the two syllables when he is startled or surprised, is very sweet when heard on a mesquite-covered hillside. The second is a little more raucous, a "kuk-kuk, kuk-kuk, kuk-kuk" starting rather low and increasing steadily in volume. It is this call that Alexander Wetmore refers to as a barking call, I think. It is sharper and more staccato than the call of either the Bobwhite or the Valley Quail, but to my ear it is not a bark. This difference of impression is to be expected, of course, because no two men react to any given bird note in the same way. Ralph Hoffman wrote of the "whinnie" of the Sora Rail, and Gayle Pickwell describes at some length the "tuck song" of the Valley Quail. I never have heard a Sora "whinnie," and, though I have lived on intimate terms with the Valley Quail all of my life, I do not know what call it is that Dr. Pickwell refers to.

In a cage, these birds are gentle and confiding, even slightly curious about what a man does as he potters about in their pen. As they move slowly and calmly about at such times, they converse with one another very pleasantly in low tones, much as do the Bobwhites in similar situations, but not so volubly. Occasionally they call loudly from the ground or from some elevated position.

One winter I noticed that the Valley Quail about my home were very little in evidence before this calling of the Scaled Quail began. After it started, they moved in on the aviary, and for the next three or four months, or until the nesting impulse entirely possessed them, they loafed about within earshot of the callers. The calls of the Valley Quail outside the cage had a somewhat similar effect on the captive Scaled Quail. Wishing to test the matter a little further, I put four native birds into the aviary with the aliens. Once together, the two species seemed to lose much of their former interest in each other. Though never antagonistic, they did not go about together within the cage, as birds of the same species inevitably would have done.

The range of the Scaled Quail, roughly, is that of the Mexican Border, as far as American hunters, who usually refer to it as the Blue Quail, are concerned, with the great bulk of the population lying to the west of the Arizona-New Mexico Line. In the bird books, all of New Mexico and the southern part of Colorado are included in this range; but I have been able to find only a relatively few quail of any species in the northern parts of either Arizona or New Mexico. A pair of Scaled Quail that I did come on one morning in the high country immediately south of Santa Fé were of considerable interest because they were in a grassy hillside where observation was a rather easy matter. I searched this neighborhood with some thoroughness for water, but found none. From this I assumed that this family would have no drinking water, except when it showered, until the young were able to fly strongly and perhaps for a much longer time.

In the southeastern portion of New Mexico, especially in and about Carlsbad, the country is very dry and very scantily covered with brush. Here the bushes may be set at intervals of ten, twenty, or thirty feet, or even more. One seems to be able to take in the whole landscape at a glance. This is an impossible habitat for quail, one might say, yet there are many quail here. Driving through this region one afternoon about three o'clock, it seemed to be evident that there was not a quail in the neighborhood. When we retraced our steps very early the next morning, however, we came on many quail as they foraged over the open ground. Wishing to test the matter a little further, we went over the same route about nine o'clock in the morning, and this time we saw only one bird, a single one perched on the top of a mesquite bush within a stone's throw of Carlsbad. This was in the summertime. It proved to us that during the hot weather the quail show their greatest activity before sunup. This observation seemed to hold for most other forms of desert animal life in this region.

Going east from Carlsbad into Texas, one comes presently to the home of the Chestnut-bellied Scaled Quail, a subspecies of the better known Scaled Quail, and one whose only difference, in the eyes of the hunter, is that it carries on its belly a dark brown patch, just as does the male of the Valley Quail. In Mexico there are other subspecies of the Scaled Quail.

In Mexico, also, is another quail that, perhaps, should be mentioned here because, though not a native of the United States, it sometimes is seen in the pens of the game farms and because several attempts to introduce it into this country have been made. This is the Elegant Quail. "Elegant" does not seem to me to be a very good name for a quail, yet I use it because I know of none better. On some game farms the bird is known as the Red Douglas, and on others as the Benson Quail. At the time that Gould painted it, it was grouped with the Scaled Quail. It was known then as "*Callipepla elegans,*" a free translation of which might be "the elegant bird with the beautiful dress." Since that time it has been reclassified, and now it is placed in the topknotted group and is known as "*Lophortyx douglasii,*" which in English is "Douglas's tasseled quail."

The Elegant Quail is a very handsome bird. Though its topknot is neither balled, nor black, as is that of the Valley Quail, it has the same number of cupped feathers—seven. In body contour it resembles the Valley Quail, but in color pattern it is wholly different, more different, in fact, than is the Mountain from the Valley Quail. Its neck, wings, and flanks are heavily washed with rich red-brown, which is the basis for its field name, "Red Douglas." Its breast is gray and its throat patch is white, speckled with black. The long plume, which curves forward very smartly, is lemon-yellow. From a distance this color pattern gives the bird a mottled appearance, while in the hand, the pattern takes definite shape and the sporty white polka dots on the red flank stand out conspicuously. These white dots make one think of the somewhat similar white dots on the sides of the cock Massena Quail, even though the former are larger and much more handsome.

When I first saw this bird, not knowing of its existence as a species, I took it to be a cross between a Valley Quail and some other bird, such a cross as one sees occasionally in collections of skins in museums. Since that day I have seen in Stokley Ligon's collection several crosses between it and other species. All were very handsome. It is to be regretted that the attempts to establish it in this country have all failed.

One morning, at the height of the mating season, another quail hunter and I went up a small branch of the Pecos River in southeastern New Mexico to a place that looked favorable for Scaled Quail. Taking seats on a rough shelf of an old lava flow that rose above the brush and overlooked the bed of the stream, we waited quietly to see if any birds would come out of the cover and show themselves. Rabbits and hares were to be seen in extraordinarily large numbers along both banks of the stream and in the tiny clearings in the cat's-claw that, for the most part, composed the brush in this arid place. It seemed to be the very peak in the population cycle of these rodents, and the country literally swarmed with them. For a little while in the early light, we watched with amusement the antics of the cottontails and the long-eared jack rabbits as they went about their business. Then a cock quail appeared on the top of a large rock just across the creek from us and began to call seductively. "Oh′-oh," he said very clearly, with his head thrown far back, "Oh′-oh, oh′-oh." He repeated this pleasant refrain many times. Then he promenaded across the top of his rock and back again, for all the world like a fat country squire with hands clasped behind his back surveying his pleasant estate from his front piazza. Coming back to his original stand, the cock took up his calling once more: "Oh′-oh, oh′-oh, oh′-oh, oh′-oh."

At this, a second cock appeared on a high, square lava block a hundred yards upstream and began to call and to promenade exactly as the first one was doing. Other birds that we could not see began to call in the brush on the hillside behind us. Then a pair of quail came out of the tangled bushes almost at our feet and, crossing the bare stones and gravel to a pool, they drank deeply.

A movement in the brush across the stream and immediately before us next caught my eye, a movement that, in the instant that I was aware of it, seemed to have been made by a long, broad, gray back. "Deer!" I thought, for I am a deer hunter too, and I never fail to be stimulated by the sight of a deer in its native cover. But when I fixed my eyes on the spot where I thought the movement had been, I saw there only two large jack rabbits that were chasing each other indolently and rather foolishly around a boulder. Then a hepatic tanager flew by us on its way upstream, its course a flaming line of red against the green of the mesquite bushes. Presently, a blue grosbeak came flying down the canyon over the creek bed. My eyes followed these brilliantly colored birds up and down again, and then, when I looked again toward the brush before me, I was startled to see there a large buck, with half-grown antlers, and a doe standing like graven images and staring fixedly at me. For some unknown reason, deer almost invariably appear suddenly to us, as if by magic. These animals were the big mule deer of the desert, "El Buro," as the natives call it. Slowly the two climbed the long hill in front of me, and presently they passed from my sight over its crest.

Coming back to the quail, I saw that the two cocks still were on their respective rocks, but the pair by the side of the pool had gone off into the brush. About this time, the sun came up over the eastern horizon and, in a little while more, the rabbits and the quail retreated into the shelter of the brush and we saw them no more. Those quail that had been calling on the hillside behind us became silent. Had we arrived at the stream bed at this time, rather than earlier, we would have said that the region was all but devoid of animal and bird life.

We returned to this pleasant spot in the late afternoon, hoping to see again many, if not most, of the interesting creatures that had showed themselves to us in the early morning, but we were disappointed. Mourning doves in some numbers came to the water to drink, flying swift and straight as these birds always do; and, in the dusk, a pair of quail flew into the stream bed from the brush of the hillside. But the quail saw us at once and refused to alight by the pool for a drink. Then a nighthawk or two appeared, seemingly from nowhere, and began to hawk over the water on long, slender wings. That was all. The really inspiring show that had been staged for us fifteen hours earlier was not repeated.

Like the Bobwhite, the Scaled Quail roosts on the ground. This is understandable when one looks across many parts of the bird's range and sees no trees large enough to serve as roosting places. The habit is of especial interest to me because I believe that it is the ground-roosting custom of the Bobwhite that is largely responsible for that bird's willingness to lie close in the presence of hunters with dogs. If the ground-roosting habit has such an effect on the character of the Bobwhite, why does it not have the same effect on the fast-running Scaled Quail? The answer to this seeming contradiction is found in the differences in cover on the two ranges, I think. The Bobwhite lives in a well-watered land of grasses and weeds and low tangles. The desert bird often lives on the almost bare ground. It can be seen at relatively long distances. In such a habitat, it not only must be continually on the move, but there is not the same degree of safety in short flight that there is for the eastern bird or for the western Valley Quail, which can, and often does, rise from the ground to the security of a dense-foliaged oak tree.

More than any other quail known to me, the Scaled Quail is open to attack by its enemies. One wonders how it eludes them all. It has seemed to me as I have gone about in its country that the ordinary quail predators are fewer in numbers here than they are elsewhere, but this may be only wishful thinking on my part. At any rate, I am sure that I have seen fewer accipiter hawks and fewer wildcats here than I have seen on other quail ranges. Even so, I tremble for the Scaled Quail each time that I come on a covey of them on the open, almost bald, desert.

The size of these coveys seems to depend on many factors: weather, food supply, cover, enemies and others. Obviously, unless the desert is unusually productive in any given place and at any given time, there cannot be those great concentrations of birds that sometimes are encountered on a Valley Quail range. Instead, the desert seems to support many small coveys rather widely scattered. In good years and in favorable places, however, the total number of birds present in some given area can be very large.

Every quail hunter, as he becomes familiar with one after another of the different species of quails, arranges them in his mind in the order in which they appeal to him. Because from the earliest time I have had it drummed into me that it is shameful to shoot a small game bird on the ground with a heavy shotgun, and because I get so much satisfaction from making cleanly a difficult wing shot, my feelings for the Scaled or Blue Quail are mixed. Unless as a camper on the desert I want a mess of quail for a meal, I get so little pleasure from shooting these birds that I do not go out on carefully planned excursions to hunt them. On the other hand, they appeal to me so greatly in every other way—their gameness, their ability to survive in a most difficult habitat, their great beauty—that I place them high on my list. Other men, with a different background of hunting, get the greatest satisfaction from pursuing and taking the Scaled Quail; and so it probably is the most widely hunted game bird in New Mexico.

8

THE BOBWHITE

Colinus virginianus

The Bobwhite is the darling of the eastern and southern woods. Undoubtedly the Ruffed Grouse is the more prized bird, from the hunter's point of view, for it is larger and it is more difficult to take for a half dozen well known reasons; yet the very qualities that make the Bobwhite the easier bird to kill are the ones that endear it most to the hunter, whether he be sportsman or farmer. This quail is an intimate, companionable bird, living from choice, as often as not, in the cultivated fields and hedges in the close vicinity of the barn. Its cheery whistle, carrying over the quiet countryside, adds warmth to the spring sunlight, and joy to the human heart that hears it.

While the Valley Quail likes best the sage-covered slopes and bottoms, the Bobwhite chooses weedy and grassy openings of the rolling uplands. Old cornfields gone to weeds are one of its favorite foraging grounds; and any cover that is not too high, where weed seeds can be gathered, and where it feels reasonably well protected from attack from above, will serve it well. It is unusual for the hunter to seek the western quail within sight of a house. The eastern quail, on the other hand, finds human habitations and all that goes with them beneficial, and so it does not look upon man with that active distrust that is so evident in the western bird.

There are many other differences that spring to the mind whenever the two species are compared. One is that the Bobwhite roosts on the ground, and almost never goes into trees. When darkness falls, the covey, so often numbering less than twenty birds, gathers on the ground in a circle, tails in and heads out, in any convenient place on its covey range, and in this formation settles down for the night. Such a spot may be used several nights in succession, but it is more usual for the covey to choose a different roosting spot each night. This nightly shifting of roosting sites is, of course, much to the advantage of the birds, otherwise the sleeping covey might be raided night after night, once their retreat was located, by the predatory hosts that are abroad between sunset and sunrise. Even as it is, with the birds constantly changing their sleeping grounds, one wonders that they do not suffer more from night prowlers than they apparently do. The life of a ground bird must be one of almost continual alarms.

Wherever seen, whether in the weeds of an old and neglected cornfield, or on the bare floor of an enclosure, the most obvious characteristics of the Bobwhite are its gentleness and its sociability. As it goes about the business of its day, it keeps up a running flow of conversational notes, very low and confidential, too low, perhaps, for most human ears, but well adapted to the purposes of the quail. Most birds and mammals that go about in flocks and herds have developed noises of one sort or another that keep the individuals informed as to the whereabouts of the central or main group. It may be that this is the chief purpose served by the low twitterings of the Bobwhite; yet it has seemed to me, as I have listened to a very small number of them talking to one another at midday, let us say, that the two or three birds present were wholly concerned with their fellows close at hand, rather than with those that were absent, for the moment, from this nucleus.

One day a boy brought me a young male, one of a number that he had raised under a bantam hen. On the way to me, something went wrong with the little box in which he carried the bird, and the quail dropped out on the sidewalk. A Valley or a Scaled Quail, in such a situation, would have been hopelessly lost to its former possessors, for it would have made off at once. The Bobwhite merely crouched on the walk until the boy had time to collect his startled wits and to put both hands softly over it. I know of nothing that speaks more eloquently of the gentleness and steadiness of the species than does this episode.

On the wing the Bobwhite, while it flushes readily enough, seems to me to fly neither as fast nor as far as does the Valley Quail. The nature of the cover it frequents and the topography of its range undoubtedly account for this difference. Other than this, the flight is typically that of a Valley Quail—a quick burst of speed attained by a great whirring of wings, and then a longer glide on stiff, horizontally-held wings to cover. This makes it a somewhat easier target for the hunter. The fact that it is found on more or less level ground, where the footing usually is good, also is in the hunter's favor.

The Bobwhite was the first quail encountered by the original settlers in this country, and has the largest range, geographically. These two facts have done much to make it by long odds the best known of our quails. For three hundred years white men have hunted it, studied it and talked about it. Surely a thousand men have followed it where one has followed any other species. A literature has sprung up about it that not only is more or less voluminous, but is searching in its detail. Many capable artists have painted it. Of these, I suppose, the first of importance was Audubon. I am well aware that it is heresy of the most dangerous kind to say anything that may be construed as derogatory to this famous naturalist painter. Yet in my opinion Audubon's portraits of our quails in general, and of the Bobwhite in particular, are among the least happy of his pictures.

There is an early picture, one of that great Currier and Ives series, which shows a pair of Bobwhite leading their family of newly hatched chicks through rather rough cover, that is a very attractive composition indeed. This seems to have appeared some years after the Audubon print, and, for some reason, is but slightly known. This print does not have all the brilliance of color that one might wish, and so it might be held by some to be a trifle dull; yet it is a charming picture, accurately drawn, and one that every bird lover who sees it must admire.

Gould did a comprehensive series of paintings of the quails of the New World. The names which he used to designate these different species do not conform very closely to those in use today, and so there may be some slight confusion on this score; but the pictures themselves are beautifully done, the birds being represented about life-size, or a trifle larger. These are among the very best prints that are available to the quail lover today; in fact, they are almost the only ones to be had. Even so, they are not easily found. Occasionally one hears of the whole series, bound in book form, being sold at auction for a considerable sum (not long ago such a volume was offered to me for $500), but the separate prints are rare.

Wishing to possess a few of these prints, notably those showing the Bobwhite of the Eastern Seaboard and the so-called Benson or Red Douglas Quail of western Mexico, I advertised rather widely for them in the proper channels. This happened near the beginning of the Second World War. To my great surprise, an answer to my advertisement came from a store in New York, saying that a shipment of these prints had just then come from London, having been sent out of England to save them from destruction by bombs. When the half dozen prints that I purchased reached me, they were in a bedraggled condition with the mats torn and badly stained. The pictures in the center, however, were unhurt. With such a history, these prints are of especial interest to me, and this interest is increased when I remember that these are the only likenesses of Mexican and Central American Quails that I have been able to find thus far.

As I look at this Gould picture of the Bobwhite, as it hangs on my wall, it seems to me a very pleasing picture even though the artist has drawn the birds so unusually round and fat and heavy.

For the hunter, I suppose there never will be painted again pictures that rank with those of A. B. Frost. It is true that he did not paint quail as such, but always as a part of a shooting scene; yet no discussion of Bobwhite pictures would be even partially complete without some mention of his work. In the main, these fine pictures all have a man or two in the foreground, a dog or two, or even three, in the middle distance, and a covey well up in the background. In many cases the birds are pictured after they have picked up speed and are gliding for cover. In one or two pictures, the dogs are focusing on a point of cover in which, it is evident, a few quail are hiding. These paintings are so true to all that makes hunting the great sport that it is, that they stand first of all among quail-hunting pictures in the minds of those who have seen them.

Fuertes, about the turn of the century and after, came into prominence as a bird illustrator. He has pictured the Bobwhite ably in all of its best known positions. One that appeals to me particularly, because it is so well done and because it shows the birds coming head on, an unusual and difficult position to portray accurately, depicts a covey that has flushed from the edge of a wood, crossed a fence, and is about to come to ground not far beyond where the observer is standing. This is a fine, animated picture, done in Fuertes's best style.

Of the many men who at present are specializing in bird portraiture and who have painted the Bobwhite, Major Allen Brooks, Lynn Bogue Hunt, William Schaldach, and Francis Lee Jaques probably are the best known. Hunt's pictures are most often seen in sporting magazines, while Brooks and Jaques most often illustrate bird books of a more or less technical nature. Kalmbach's work can be seen in Stoddard's encyclopedic volume on the Bobwhite. Although so many men have painted the quails, especially the Bobwhite, it is, unfortunately, very difficult for the quail lover to purchase a good print, done in permanent colors, of any American quail.

From all this it will be seen that around the Bobwhite an extensive literature has grown up. Almost completely, this is a sportsman's literature, written and illustrated by them and for them. Whatever protection the birds have received has come, for the most part, from the same source. This is a matter that is not well understood by bird lovers in general, if we exclude from this group the active shooters and hunters, or, for that matter, by many of the hunters themselves. It was the sportsmen of the East and South, for example, that made Stoddard's study of the Bobwhite possible. And it has been the well informed sportsman who shoots regularly every season who has been responsible for most game protection laws, even laws of a drastic nature. Left to their own devices, few legislatures would bother about legislative acts of this sort. It is also true that when bag limits are made too low many men cease to hunt, hunting clubs go out of business, and the poacher and pothunter take over the field. The latter often use nets and gins instead of guns, and take literally thousands, where tens were taken before they came on the field. It seems to be even more impossible to keep down an illicit commerce in game birds, once the sportsman ceases to interest himself actively in the matter, than it was to keep down the trade in bootleg liquor in the days of prohibition.

To western hunters, it appears that a cult is forming around the Bobwhite, the cult of the shooter. As I see it, free hunting is a thing of the past over much of this bird's range. The quail has been killed off over large areas by human agencies, among which hunters are but one. The coveys that now remain are for the most part on land where shooting is entirely prohibited, or where it is strictly limited to the owners and tenants. Under these conditions, to which, by the way, the Pacific Coast surely is coming, some fortunately situated land-owners still have good quail-shooting at little or no cost, just as they always have had; others, by a more or less moderate outlay, can have good shooting if they wish it; and still others now have shooting only after considerable outlay of money. For this last group, land must be rented, keepers must be paid, and the coveys must be cultivated before the sportsman can hope to do much in the way of shooting.

In the cultivation of the quail, there are two methods that usually are employed in whole or in part. Under one of these methods, every effort is made to protect the native stock and to insure its increase. Vermin, such as rats, cats, skunks, foxes, and hawks, are assiduously trapped and shot. Suitable cover is carefully provided, and various food crops are planted for the use of the Bobwhite. Under the other method, large numbers of foreign birds are imported from other territories, especially from Texas.

The foreign birds are purchased in lots by the hundred and even by the thousand. Often both plans are put in practice on the same plantation, the foreign birds being used as a reinforcement to the native birds; and the success of the interbreeding is carefully watched. Having gone this far, a good kennel on the rented ground becomes the next essential, for it is obviously foolish to forego the pleasure of hunting with dogs in country and with birds that make their employment practical. Indeed, I can think of no greater pleasure that the hunting field has to offer than that of hunting over well trained dogs. Many a man takes the field for little else than the satisfaction of seeing these intelligent creatures work through the coverts.

The shooting itself, under these more or less artificial conditions, tends to become formalized. Rules of procedure tend to become worked out in detail, and the whole business may take on some of the aspects of a social affair. On some preserves, for example, it has seemed necessary each time that there is a shoot to divide the land to be shot over into as many squares as there are shooters. The night before the shoot, keepers drop a certain predetermined number of birds from the cages here and there about each square. As these birds are put out in the darkness, most of them stay where they are dropped until the arrival of the dogs and shooters next morning.

To the old-fashioned hunters, such refinements as these may seem to make the shooting too easy, and to rob it of much of its zest and virility. To accept such rules hastily at their face value, however, would be unfair both to the men who make them and to the men against whom they are levied; for neither group is in a position sympathetically to understand the position of the other. It is merely a question of each one getting his sport where he finds it. For my part, I have every smypathy for the man who thoroughly enjoys a day in the rolling uplands with a gun in his hand, and who is willing to pay handsomely, either in energy or money or both, for such a day. The deciding factor is, I think, not under what conditions a man hunts or how much game he brings home, but rather what appreciation he has of the out-of-doors and what satisfactions a good shoot brings to him. Occasionally one meets a man who seems to have little love of the out-of-doors and no interest in or admiration for the game birds that he kills, even though he prides himself on his skill as a shot and his knowledge of and conformity with the niceties of the shooting field. The true outdoorsman can have little patience with such a person.

One fall a man of this type came to Santa Barbara. All his life he had hunted and shot under the most artificial conditions, but he had heard of the gameness of the Valley Quail and wished to try his skill on the bird. We went out together, and we had a fine, large day of it in the coastal foothills. It was hard work, of course, and it was great sport. On our return to the car, my acquaintance carefully counted his bag and mine, and when he found that I had three more birds than he had, he offered me $15 from his pocketbook. I was completely mystified by this procedure, for I could not think what prompted it. Seeing this, he explained to me that the men of his shooting club commonly shot for $5 the bird, and that he supposed that the same custom held in California. This was a new experience to me, and a somewhat exasperating one; I cannot see that the putting of money on the outcome of a shoot adds anything in pleasure to that shoot—for true sportsmen it detracts a great deal. For my part I should as soon buy my game outright from the butcher as shoot for it at $5 the bird.

In its nesting habits the Bobwhite is of unusual interest, for in a number of cases, it builds a canopy of woven grass stems over its nest. The eggs of the Bobwhite are almost pure white. When not being brooded by the hen, they are particularly noticeable to any eye searching for them. Ordinarily, this would be less of a danger than might be expected because most of the prowlers are controlled by scent rather than sight. However, they do notice even motionless objects when the contrast in color is obvious as in the case of the eggs of the Bobwhite. The hood, therefore, which can be compared to the hood over a bassinet, acts as a screen and greatly cuts down the visibility of the eggs.

Two habits of the Bobwhite, that of roosting on the ground, and that of lying so close in the near presence of a bird dog, are of the greatest interest to me. As I consider them, it seems that they are closely related. At night, for example, as a covey squats motionless on the ground and hears the approach of some other creature, how nice a calculation must be made by the birds! Obviously, none of them wishes to flush and go off through the darkness. Such a course has many of the gravest hazards for the bird that follows it. To run from the spot probably would be more dangerous by far than to fly. On the other hand, the birds cannot sit tight until the unseen prowler, whatever it is, is upon them. To do that would be certain death. When is the time to rise? How much longer can the birds afford to squat motionless in the hope that the prowler will pass them by unnoticed? It seems to me that it is this habit of ground-roosting in close cover that is largely responsible for the Bobwhite's tendency to lie so very close at all times.

Because the Bobwhite goes about in such small flocks and because it lies so well to a dog, the method of hunting it is very different from that used in hunting western quails. When a flock of a dozen birds, let us say, is found by the dogs, the hunter approaches the spot where they are located and, when he is ready, flushes them. Those that remain after the first rise and fire scatter much as Mearns's Quail do in the same situation and come to ground at not too great distances from the flushing point. These are carefully marked down by the hunter, and as single birds they then can be systematically sought out. With some luck to aid the keen-scented dogs, almost every one of these birds can be found. This means that the hunters must curb their appetites, lest they destroy the entire covey in one encounter. The fact that there are so few birds in a single covey, often not more than the parents and those of the brood that have survived the many dangers that have beset them during their adolescence, makes it probable that there are several other coveys in the near neighborhood. A man is more likely, therefore, to leave a covey after he has shot from it three or four birds and to go in search of others, than he would be if he thought that these were the only birds that he was likely to encounter that day.

It is hard to set a standard for measuring accurately the keenness of scent in a hunting dog. We may feel that this setter is keener than that pointer, or visa versa; but we are unable accurately to say by how much. Every man, I suppose, likes to remember the unusual finds that his particular dog has made for him, for the average shooter loves his dog—usually is proud of the animal even though, in the estimation of others, the beast is a proven fool. Many are the remarkable stories that sportsmen have to tell. What seems to me the most remarkable feat a good dog performs is that of picking up on the air the scent of a quail that has been seen in flight minutes before the dog arrived on the scene. Most hunters have seen a dog do this often, I suppose.

Whether we are able to measure his nose accurately or not, it is an accepted fact that a good dog has little trouble in locating a Bobwhite once he comes reasonably close to where the bird lies. This ability on the part of the dog places the quail at the mercy of the sportsman.

My own conclusion is that the sportsman, if he would hunt the Bobwhite with the maximum of satisfaction, must be a gentleman of the old school, one with an instinctive sympathy with all those niceties of the hunting field that are the heritage not of the rich, the well-born, and the able, but only of the elect; that he must be one who hunts leisurely and with as keen an interest in leaving unharmed the larger parts of the coveys found as he is in filling his bag. More than this, he must have some knowledge of the birds he shoots and of the history of the country over which he hunts.

A half dozen Bobwhites make a bag of which to be proud. These quail are so beautifully colored, the red washing and the patterns on the individual feathers are so pleasing, that it is a delight to hold one of them in the hand and to examine its plumage.

9

THE MASKED BOBWHITE

Colinus ridgwayi

The Masked Bobwhite is a quail interesting out of all proportion to its numbers, or to the size of its range. By every criterion except that of color, it is a true Bobwhite; yet its color pattern, especially in the male, at once sets it apart from its famous relative. It is the handsomest of the Bobwhites of the United States, a red fellow with a black face that is not as noticeably a mask as is the similar black area on the Lawrence's Goldfinch, and yet one that sets off beautifully the red-brown head, breast and back.

This is the first of the so-called red Bobwhites that the hunter meets as he journeys south into Mexico. On these birds the red washing extends from the head down the chest and back to the tail. This gives them an unusually striking appearance, especially when they take wing, and the sun, striking their plumage fully, gives it an even ruddier glow. Another red Bobwhite of the south is *Colinus graysoni.* The throat patch of this species is white and not black, an interesting and significant variation. When the visitor considers these red birds, together with the red phase of the eastern Bobwhite, there is opened to him an especially interesting field for speculation. Speaking generally, little is known of why birds are colored as they are. Certain areas of the plumage seem to lend themselves especially to brilliant pigmentation. The throat seems to be the most important of these, and here, on one species or another, almost every color of the rainbow can be found. To mention only several, some warblers have yellow throats, and others have black throats. The house finch is red here, and the mountain bluebird is blue. Another area of brilliant coloration is the rump, and a third and fourth are the crown of the head and flanks.

The color pattern of all these red Bobwhites seems to indicate in this genus a strong tendency toward erythrism (excessive redness). Albinism is more or less common in all animal forms, and every hunter, at one time or another, encounters evidences of it in the birds and mammals which he sees in the field. Melanism, the tendency toward dark or black plumage, is less frequently noticed, though it is fairly common among certain of the hawks. Erythrism, however, has received but little consideration up to the present, and, as a consequence, little is known about it. Several common forms, the ordinary screech owl for example, have a red color phase as well as the more usual gray one. Little or nothing is known about the causes of this dichromatic tendency in either owls or quails. The fact that there are recognized species of the Bobwhite that, to the casual eye, appear to resemble closely the red phase of the eastern bird adds greatly to the interest of the matter.

In former days the Masked Quail was found in the United States in some numbers, especially in the area around Globe, Arizona. The bird books tell us that it has been driven from this region now, and has been forced to retreat to the rough and dry region south of the Mexican Border; but it seems to me that it would be more accurate to say that it has been exterminated from that part of its range within Arizona. Those birds of this species that now are found in Mexico are the descendants of others that always have lived in that region. The cause of the quail's disappearance from south-central Arizona seems to have been the destruction of its cover there, fully as much as its slaughter by powder and shot.

In Mexico, that land of no game laws, the species may still thrive in numbers sufficient to maintain a modest traffic in the birds across the line, yet the number of birds there seems to be declining steadily. An incident in this traffic, related to me by one of the participants in it, is of sufficient interest to warrant retelling. Moved by one of those generous impulses that occasionally possess the young and inexperienced, a small group of enthusiastic hunters in Arizona came to the conclusion that the Masked Quail never should have been allowed to die out in their state, and that something should be done at once toward restocking the empty coverts. Though none of these young men was receiving more than $4 or $5 a day in wages, they readily agreed to pool what money they had on hand, and to import as many Masked Quail from Mexico as this modest fund would buy. Older men would have hesitated to embark on so ambitious a venture with so small a capital, but these fellows were not disturbed by the several obvious risks and difficulties inherent in such an undertaking, nor did it occur to them that the first move in restocking must be the restoration of a suitable cover. They at once got in touch with a man below the Border who could and would supply them with the quail, and they procured the necessary permits to get the shipment across the line. Every obstacle seemed to have been successfully surmounted, and already they looked forward to the time when there would be sufficient numbers of the progeny of these first birds to make an open season on them safe and practicable. In high spirits, therefore, they went to meet the consignment at the designated point of importation. But at this place a difficulty arose to dash their exuberant spirits. For reasons that were not altogether clear to the Americans, the Mexican officials refused to allow the birds to leave Mexican soil. Though one may surmise what was the cause of this sudden change of face on the part of the officials, all that could be said surely was that the young men would not be given possession of the quail. In the argument that followed much was said that need not be repeated here, for the Americans were young and impulsive, and they did not take kindly to the idea that they were to be thwarted in so patriotic and right an enterprise as the one in which they were engaged. At last, however, when it became clear that further argument was useless, they determined to make the best of a bad job. The argument was renewed with vigor, and as one of their number engaged the attention of the officials, the surreptitious hand of another opened the door of the crate. In a moment the quail were out of the crate and were whirring off to the nearest cover. What happened to the birds after this my informant did not know, but he hoped that they had survived and already had begun to multiply in numbers sufficient to cause them to spread to the north. So generous an enterprise certainly deserved a more successful conclusion.

Almost the only place north of the Border where a quail of this species is to be seen today is in a case in a museum. Most of these mounted skins are old now, because they were taken, for the most part, many years ago, and their once-bright plumage is sadly faded. One such mounted specimen that I saw a few years ago in Chicago still lingers pathetically in my memory because there was so little about it to suggest the truly beautiful bird it once was when it ran and foraged and mated in lively mood through the sunlit grass of its native coverts in Arizona.

A few game breeders still have small pens of these birds, but not many. Sometimes they can be purchased at a price about five times that of the Scaled Quail. Nowhere are they numerous any more. The prevailing opinion seems to be that they are all but extinct.

In the late winter of the year 1947 I purchased a pair of Masked Bobwhites from a dealer in Los Angeles for $25. This would seem to be a high price to anyone not familiar with the present status of the species. From the breeder's point of view, however, it was reasonable because he did not know where any others could be obtained. Even in Mexico there was no known supply left for importation.

Through observing this pair, the last that I expect to see alive, as they lived quietly in their cage, and through corresponding with the breeder, I learned several interesting facts. The first of these is that the young birds show considerable variation in the facial markings. The cock, when he came to me, had a small but noticeable white line near the base of the black shield or mask. Now, after six months, this is all but gone. There is also much variation in the white line over the eye. Some birds have this superorbital line and some do not. Secondly, in a reasonably good cage, this species lays from twenty to sixty eggs each year, and it lives for about seven years. And thirdly, no other quail known to me, with the possible exception of the Massena Quail, merges so nearly perfectly with the bare ground about it when it squats. Even in so small a cage, where I could not help knowing the birds' approximate location, I failed to make them out time and time again until one or the other of them moved. In a general way, the markings on this quail's back are arranged in a pattern similar to those on the back of the Massena Quail.

One of the most pleasing characteristics of these two caged birds is their tameness and gentleness. Though wild when they came to me, they soon calmed down. In three months they were as quiet and tame in my presence as a pair of common Bobwhites might have been in the same situation.

The eggs of the Masked Bobwhite are of interest to anyone who seeks to trace relationships among the birds by this means. Among the quails of the United States, taken as a group, the eggs move step by step from the white eggs of the eastern Bobwhite to the speckled, chocolate ones of the western Mountain Quail. In this series, the Masked Bobwhite's eggs are the second from the white end, and those of the Valley Quail are the second from the dark end.

The Masked Bobwhite is so much like the common Bobwhite in voice and habits, and so very unlike it in color pattern, that not only the layman but the systematist as well is perplexed to know where to place the bird in the scheme of living creatures. Is this a species in its own right, or is it merely a subspecies of the common bird? On the one hand is the color pattern of the male which, certainly, is very different from that of the Common Bobwhite. On this basis, the bird books in which it is described have given it full species status and have named it "*Colinus ridg-*

wayi." On the other hand are the similarity in color pattern of the females of the two kinds, the almost identical call notes and habits, and the fact that the common Bobwhite is known to have a strong tendency toward erythrism. Weighing all the evidence carefully, Dr. Peters now definitely classes the masked bird as a subspecies of the common one, and he gives it the name of "*Colinus virginianus ridgwayi.*"

My own opinion in this very interesting discussion, which, by the way, is worth very little because I am only a hunter, is not clearly formed. The preponderance of evidence certainly supports James Lee Peters, I think. Yet the great difference in color pattern of the males of the two kinds is an obstacle over which I leap with difficulty. Perhaps the wisest course is to fall back on the right of the hunter to give to any bird in the field the name that seems to him to be the most suitable, and to leave to the systematist the joy of deciding the finest points in the bird's relationships. On this basis, I have given the Masked Bobwhite at the head of this chapter the name by which it is known in most textbooks; and on the chart, which appears on page xiii, I show it as Dr. Peters would have me do.

10

TRANSPLANTING AND RESTOCKING

Almost every sportsman at one time or another interests himself in plans for the introduction of new game birds into his neighborhood or with schemes for the restocking of shot-out coverts with native birds from another district.

The bird known to the British as the "Gray Partridge," and to American sportsmen as the "Hungarian Partridge," has been introduced in this country with some success. It is a big, strong bird twice as large as any one of our native quails, with the possible exception of the Mountain Quail. Though clearly a partridge and not a quail, it has many quail-like qualities and habits. Like most members of this group, it is a fast flyer. In my opinion, based admittedly on insufficient data, it is faster on the wing than any of our American quails. At any rate, this much is certain: a large bird seems to go at a slower pace than does a small one. If it is held generally by gunners that the Gray Partridge is as fast, at least, as the Bobwhite, which is the generally held opinion, it can be said with assurance that, were it possible to clock the two flyers, the larger one would be found to be flying at a considerably higher speed.

As an illustration of this fact, one morning when I was out in a fast and powerful speedboat that could do fifty miles an hour and better, I was unable to come up with a large cormorant that was flying close to the surface of the ocean above the relatively quiet water just inside the kelp line. When first sighted, this bird was standing on a floating log, and it flushed at about a hundred yards. I chased it for a considerable distance but was unable to cut down its lead. This incident proved conclusively to me that appearances can be deceptive when moving objects are considered. Up to this time, I had classed this bird as a slow flyer, certainly a much slower flyer than a duck—and this in spite of the fact that I had had the best possible opportunity to study the bird. I had watched ducks with the keenest interest, as every other hunter must have done. I knew, for example, that it can be proved easily and with reasonable certainty by keeping one's car abreast of a flying flock as one drives along the paved highway that crosses this extensive marsh that scaup commonly fly over the marshes of lower San Francisco Bay at a speed of about fifty-five miles an hour. Putting these two speeds together, it becomes evident that, all appearances to the contrary, the large cormorant flies almost as fast as does the small duck.

To go back to the quails, the Mountain Quail seems to me to be the fastest flyer of our quails; but this opinion is held only tentatively. There are so many difficulties to overcome here before an accurate check can be made! First of all, the Mountain Quail seldom is in the air long enough for it to reach its maximum speed. Secondly, it almost never flies over level land for the simple reason that the region where it is found usually is a steeply tilted one. Under these conditions, the actual speed at which it is able to fly when pressed is a matter of conjecture. Admitting all this, I still maintain that it is the fastest flyer found among our native quails. In much the same way, I feel that the Gray Partridge is faster than the Mountain Quail.

The Gray Partridge is a handsome bird. Looking at it either in the hand or on the ground, one can understand easily why it is the favorite of the English countryman and gunner. Because of its great popularity in England, most of our information about the bird, up to the last decade or two, has come from that country, though the species is native to most of Europe. The color pattern is wholly different from that of our quails. It is a combination of browns and grays, with much barring or heavy lining on the back and flanks. In this latter trend it is more suggestive of the markings of the prairie chicken than it is of the markings of the Bobwhite or the Valley Quail.

Structurally, too, there are obvious differences between the birds. When put in a pen with our native birds, not only does the superior size of the Partridge at once become noticeable, but many other differences spring to the eye. Its air of alertness, of superior strength, and its heavy, long, deadly bill are obvious. This is a hardy bird, the observer is convinced, and one that is well able to fend for itself.

Walter E. Collinge, in "The Food of Some British Game Birds," sets the animal content of the food eaten by this partridge at 40.5 per cent of the whole. This must come as a surprise to quail shooters in general, when first they hear about it, because it is known that the Bobwhite consumes only about 14 per cent of animal food, as an average for the year, and the Valley Quail, almost a strict vegetarian, only 3.5 per cent. The Gray Partridge ranks ahead of even the common pheasant in this regard, for the latter, though a famous eater of ants and other insects, averages only about 37 per cent of animal food in its diet. When one considers the shape and size of the Partridge's bill, however, so different from that of one of our quails, this high percentage of animal food in its diet is to be expected.

According to English sporting books, many years ago it was the custom of gunners to walk up the partridges in the stubble, and this still is done to a limited extent. Then the drive method of shooting was instituted on the large estates. This system presupposes a line of ten or a dozen shooters stationed at predetermined and carefully selected stands in the open, and a line of beaters who attempt to drive the birds over the stands from the cover where they have been feeding and loafing. Such a drive may include both English and French partridges. On a good day, three hundred to five hundred birds may be killed by the line of gunners, but only one or two such drives are practicable in a season. The shooting is all head-on and fairly high, the exact opposite of what it is when the partridges are walked up.

Very many attempts have been made to introduce this fine game bird into the United States. No accurate record of these attempts has been kept, and so it is not possible now to know what proportion of them has been successful and what part failures. Probably the failures have far exceeded the successes. In many cases the cover into which the birds have been liberated has not been suitable. The climate in other places has been unfavorable. In some other instances, however, the introducers have met with marked success. Generally, the Gray Partridge has thrived in those regions where there are extensive grain fields and where the climate is sufficiently humid to nourish a suitable cover for the birds after the grain is harvested. In some parts of Oregon, this partridge has established itself in sufficient numbers to be classed as a fairly common resident. When I drove along the main state highway in an automobile as early as the year 1924, I saw them there at the side of the road.

It is in the great central valleys of the continent, however, that the Gray Partridge has found conditions most favorable, and there it has become thoroughly established and has multiplied to the complete satisfaction of the most optimistic sportsman. In a certain sense, it can be said to be taking the place of the fast-disappearing prairie chicken in these grain fields. Accustomed for centuries to living on rather closely built-up farm lands, it seems to be able to increase its hold on American fields that are too much used by man for the continuance there of the wilder prairie chicken. Even in the rigorous climate of the southern Canadian provinces, the Gray Partridge has done very well indeed.

In California, where we have every climate from subtropical to arctic, we have made repeated attempts to introduce this or that foreign species of game bird, and the same thing can be said of many other states. In the great majority of cases these efforts of ours have met with complete failure. Pheasants, to take one species, have been liberated over and over again in most parts of the state. Though there is today a huge pheasant population in the rice fields of the Sacramento Valley, and though there are enough birds in the Owens Valley to make it worth while for the hunter to seek them there, the rest of the state is by no means so fortunate. Generally speaking, the whole of southern California has proved to be too dry for them.

The same thing might be said of our attempts to have the Gray Partridge take hold here. There is this important difference between the two species, however: nowhere has the partridge been able to establish itself as the pheasant has done in the Sacramento Valley. There are two small areas where the birds seem to be holding their own, and that is all. Visiting the state game farm at Chino in the year 1934, I was told by the manager that twenty thousand birds already had been, or were definitely planned to be, liberated throughout the state. When I visited this same farm in 1947, I did not see a single partridge on the premises. By that time the experiment had been recognized as all but a failure, and so it had been discontinued.

There have been several attempts made to introduce the Elegant Quail, sometimes known as the Benson Quail, and again as the Red Douglas, into this state, a bird formerly classed with the Scaled Quails, and now put into the Valley and Desert quails group. This is an exceptionally handsome bird, a native of that arid region lying to the south of the Mexican Border and to the east of the Gulf of California. Inasmuch as certain areas within California are not dissimilar to this Mexican region in climate and cover, it was thought that the attempt was well worth trying. If it succeeded, certainly a fine game bird would have been added to our list; and, if it failed, no great harm would have been done. The attempts did not succeed. The liberated birds simply went off and were not seen again.

Similarly, attempts have been made along the Eastern Seaboard to introduce the Common or Migratory Quail of Europe, Asia, and Africa. This is the quail that probably is referred to in the Bible when, according to the account in the Book of Exodus, the starving Hebrews came on a great migration of the birds in the Wilderness of Sinai. These attempts at introduction also failed. Some men believe that the probable reason for the failures was that the birds, when the migratory instinct took possession of them, flew out over the Atlantic Ocean and were lost. Whether this is so or not, it is certain that there are no members of this interesting species in the United States today. Like so many other members of this great group, birds of this species lay up to eighteen eggs at a sitting, though the usual number is seven to twelve. From this it would seem that the species would have increased rapidly if once successfully introduced here.

Most men interested in the subject realize that introductions of alien stocks should be made cautiously and only after the most careful study of all species involved in any given attempt. Quite aside from the probable waste of time, money and effort, there are certain risks and dangers inherent in all such activities. There is, first of all, the ever-present danger of introducing some new and deadly disease into the native coveys when birds from another land are set free. As an example of this danger, consider the case against the ordinary barnyard chicken. Coccidiosis, to name only one ailment, is prevalent among chickens. Poultrymen, to their sorrow, are well acquainted with it, and they are untiring in their efforts to keep it under control. To the individual chicken it may or may not prove fatal, but to a flock as a whole this is not so. To the quail that range in the immediate vicinity of the barn on the ordinary ranch, however, it is as deadly as was chicken pox to the American Indians when the Whites, coming to this continent, first introduced the disease. Many a rancher, at the outset of his career, has noticed with pleasure the fact that the quail have come out of the brush and have fed with his chickens in the barnyard. Then, after a while, if his perceptions are acute, he has noticed that the quail no longer have held to this pleasant practice. Probably he has attributed the disappearance of the quail to some unknown agent that has come along either to scare them away or to kill them. The truth probably is that while cats have caught some of the quail and hawks have taken a few others, coccidiosis accounted for the great bulk of them.

I was interested to note, when I visited the ably run game farm in Carlsbad, New Mexico, that the manager, Mr. James Cox, would not allow anyone about his quail pens who previously had been near a chicken coop, because he feared that disease would be brought to his birds on the soles of his visitors' shoes. Considering these facts, it becomes evident to every sportsman that unless the greatest care is taken and extensive studies are made no one can be sure that diseases deadly to the native stock may not be introduced into the country when a new species is liberated there.

There is a further danger that usually goes unnoticed by the average sportsman: a new species, if conditions are favorable for it, not only will take root and thrive, but in the end will surplant or drive out the native bird that corresponds to it and with whom it is in competition. In the non-game field, one has but to consider the English Sparrow or the starling to see how devastating to the native birds the introduction of a new species may be. It is laid down as a law of nature by some ornithologists that no two species of birds can occupy exactly the same niche for long. In the end, one will drive out the other, or the weaker one, unable to maintain itself, will perish. In the United States, so far, no introduced game bird has driven out a native game bird, but we have no assurance that such an unhappy thing cannot occur in the future.

Insofar as I have been able to discover, the Gray Partridge does not compete at the present time with any of our native quails. This bird is a creature of more northern climates, whereas our quails were evolved in warmer regions, and seem to shun the colder latitudes. Speaking generally, the farther south one goes on this continent, the more different species of quails are seen and, oftentimes, the more birds there are of each species. The number of different species and subspecies of native quails in Mexico is almost legion. North of Mexico this great wealth becomes less and less the farther one goes. New Mexico has five kinds of quails native to it, Arizona has four, California and Texas have three, and the states to the north and east have but one, the Bobwhite, until, in our most northern latitudes, no native quail is found. Into this distribution picture the Gray Partridge fits very well. It apparently does not like the hot weather of the Mexican Border, and it thrives in northern areas where the temperatures at times are so cold that all other bare legged, nonmigrating fowls but the pheasant are frozen out. As far north as the wheat fields of central Canada it is abundant. It is an astonishing circumstance that all these northern birds, seemingly, are sprung from a single liberation of eight hundred individuals.

As stated earlier, in the British Isles, this bird goes by the name of the "Gray Partridge," or, sometimes, the "English Partridge"; while the bird we know as the Chukar is called by the British the "French Partridge" or the "Red Leg." In the United States, the former has come to be called universally the "Hungarian Partridge" because so many importations originated in Hungary. In the field, many if not most hunters now know it simply as the "Hun." Whether ornithologists and systematists like this abbreviation or not, this seems to be the name by which the bird ultimately will be known in this country. So long as it is remembered that knowledge of the bird does not come to us in the first instance either from Germany or Hungary, "Hun" will serve very well. European Partridge is an unfortunate name for it because there are other partridges equally deserving of the title there.

Wishing to study the Gray Partridge at close quarters, I purchased a pair and put them in a large aviary with other fowls. With such birds as Valley and Desert quails they got along very well. At any rate, there was no such fighting and persecution as there is when Valley Quail are cooped with pheasants. Each species tolerated the other, though the larger birds seemed to be much tamer and less nervous than the smaller ones. Then I introduced into the cage some Bamboo Quail, and at once there was trouble. The partridges seemed to dislike or resent the presence of the Bamboo Quail very much, and they pecked viciously at them whenever the little birds ventured too close. The aviary was large enough to permit the two species to live comfortably together if the partridges had behaved decently. One after another the little quails were killed by these deadly pecks, and in a day or two all were gone. Once a Bamboo Quail was killed, the partridges cleaned the carcass of flesh.

In nesting habits the Gray Partridge is much like our quails. It lays as many as eighteen eggs and, on carefully preserved ground, it manages to bring to maturity an average of about six chicks. Under wholly wild conditions, it will not do as well as this, perhaps, yet it will do well enough to show large increases in areas favorable to it. Like the Bobwhite, it often goes about in coveys of ten or a dozen birds, with the coveys, where the birds are numerous, not widely scattered. A thirty-bird covey is a large one. From every standpoint, this is a fine game bird, a valued addition to our native quails and grouses.

What has been said about the English Gray Partridge applies with almost equal force to the so-called "Chukar," the "French Partridge" or "Red Leg" of the British sporting books. There is this important difference, however: the Chukar has found conditions much less to its liking in the United States than has the Hungarian. This is amply demonstrated in the present game laws. The Hungarian appears a dozen times in these lists printed state by state and territory by territory, and the Chukar not once.

It is widely believed that the Chukar will not nest in captivity and that it does so only sparingly when liberated. So far as my information goes, this is an individual matter with the birds. For example, I photographed a hen Chukar that had escaped from her pen in the North Hollywood Game Farm and, remaining in the immediate vicinity, had made a nest in the weeds and briars under a fence. At the time of my visit, she was incubating her eggs as faithfully as a bantam hen.

Here in the West, the peak of Chukar liberations was the decade between 1925 and 1935. In 1947, this bird was noticeable for its almost total absence on the state-managed game farms, nor is it often offered for sale in advertisements in the sporting magazines.

Looking at the business of transplanting game birds from the opposite point of view, that is, from the point of view of the success that has attended efforts to stock foreign areas with our birds and to restock exhausted areas in this country, the impression given to the student is wholly different. It is true that the efforts to introduce the Bobwhite into England have failed in every instance, but those to introduce the Valley Quail into far corners of the earth have succeeded famously. There are Valley Quail now in Hawaii and other islands of the Pacific area, and in the United States this species as well as the Bobwhite, has been planted successfully in many places far removed from its native sagebrush. Visiting a friend in Tacoma, Washington, for example, it was a pleasure to see a flock of these birds feeding on the lawn near the heart of the city, and to hear them calling from the shrubbery.

In the Salinas Valley near the community of Shandon, a rancher deeply interested in hunting decided to restock a patch of brush on his ranch that in past years had served as a range for a considerable flock of Valley Quail but that now was empty. Excessive shooting, together with other unfortunate happenings, had annihilated the quail to the last bird. Food and cover still were there, making the effort involved in replacing the birds worth while. Having killed as many enemies that habitually prey on quail as he could, he secured a dozen pairs of young Valley Quail from a game farm and liberated them in 1945. In the fall of 1946, he was able to count fifty birds in the now greatly increased covey. In the early summer of the following year, after but two nesting seasons, there were in the flock about 150 birds. Quite reasonably, he was greatly elated by this success. Then a wild domestic cat appeared on the scene, and, before its presence became known, reduced the covey by at least 10 per cent.

The conclusions that can be drawn from this single, carefully watched effort at restocking are of considerable interest. The first of these is that the quails, because of the large number of eggs in each clutch, are capable of great and quick recoveries whenever and wherever on their native range they are given proper food and shelter and protection from their numerous enemies. The second conclusion is that very little effort is required in successful restocking projects, nor is much money involved in them. Native birds usually can be obtained without charge through some state agency, or, where this is not the case, they can be purchased relatively cheaply at commercial game farms. Also, it may be concluded that young birds are essential to such projects. It is a widely held belief that old birds are not as prolific as young ones and they are not as easily and as cheaply handled. This incident illustrates very well, too, the deadliness of the wild domestic cat as a quail hunter. Because of its small size, it can go almost anywhere that a quail can go in the brush, something that its larger relative, the bobcat, cannot do. For the most part, the quail are defenseless against it during the sunlit hours that they are on the ground. I rank the tame cat gone wild as the deadliest so-called natural enemy that the Valley Quail has to face.

The considered opinion of many men long experienced in game conservation is that it is wiser to concentrate on the preservation and the increasing of the game that is native to our cover than it is to look abroad for new species to be introduced here. The most important single feature of this program, especially in the West, is the reestablishment of a sufficient cover—cover where the birds will find not only shelter, but an abundant supply of food. Heavily grazed land makes an impossible range for game birds.

11

RANDOM OBSERVATIONS

One of the most important factors in the continuing existence of a covey of quail is the span of life of the average individual. Obviously, it is not possible to arrive at a figure that is absolutely accurate; yet, by considering what data is available, a fairly reliable estimate can be made.

One spring day a friend of mine found a newly hatched Valley Quail chick and, taking it into the house and caring for it in a cage there, she was able to keep it alive for nine years. At the end of that time the bird, a hen, was so decrepit that it could no longer stand on its feet, and had to be killed. It was apparent to all of us, however, that this bird, had it been unprotected and in a wild state, would have fallen to one or another of its enemies years before this final helpless condition overtook it. Herbert L. Stoddard gives about the same longevity for Bobwhites in pens on the Eastern Seaboard. A game breeder in southern California believes that a Masked Bobwhite in one of his breeding coops lives to an age of from six to eight years. Taking these examples from three widely scattered species, and considering them to be more or less typical of the quail group as a whole, it seems to me that the best a quail, which has come safely through the many hazards of the first four months of its existence, can hope for is a life span of five years. This is not a very long period, yet many competent men hold that a smaller figure is more likely to be correct.

To estimate the probable increase in numbers in a flock of Valley Quail, we shall use the five-year life span as a basis. A flock of this species that arrives at the opening of the breeding season with a hundred birds was no very great flock some years ago, and even today there are many places where flocks of this size can be found. As one hundred is an easy and convenient number with which to work, it seems wise to use a flock of this size as a basis for our calculations. Of these one hundred individuals, the males will be in the majority. There may be fifty-three or fifty-four cocks and not more than forty-six or forty-seven hens. It is a fair assumption for the purposes of discussion that there will be at least forty-five pairs that are prepared to nest. Of these forty-five pairs, however, not all of them, by any means, will be successful in incubating their eggs and in bringing off broods of chicks. In a good year, probably one half may nest and brood without molestation. In a very bad year, not as many as one tenth may bring off chicks. In an average year, one third of the number of pairs in a flock may hatch out their eggs successfully.

Taking one third as the probable figure, some two hundred twenty-five baby quail will be produced in an average spring in a flock of one hundred birds. Of this host, how many will reach maturity during the next five or six months? Many an outdoorsman will have information here that is pertinent, for most of them have seen, at one time or another, broods of young quail with their parents, and have noticed how drastically the numbers of the little ones have shrunk as spring has turned into summer and summer has lengthened toward early fall. In an average brood the actual number of chicks that manage to escape destruction until October can only be guessed at, of course. Probably it varies from year to year and is different in each species. It happens that the few Mountain Quail families that I have seen were large—that they had been able to maintain the family circle almost intact. I am confident that this good fortune is not common to the species as a whole. On the other hand, the half-grown broods of Valley Quail that I have seen usually have been reduced to four, five, or six chicks after only a month or two of existence. A few have numbered as many as eight, but others of which I have had knowledge from the time they left the nests, have disappeared to the last chick long before October and the open hunting season came along. Occasionally in midsummer I have encountered two or more pairs with reduced progeny that have joined forces, and when this has occurred, it has been impossible for me to know accurately what losses each pair has suffered. Usually these groups have had in them an uneven number of old birds and chicks of at least two different sizes. I suppose that it is from this last-mentioned circumstance that the stubbornly held belief has arisen that the male Valley Quail incubates the first clutch of eggs laid by the female, and that the female then makes a new nest and in it incubates a second clutch of eggs.

Considering all the information available to me, I have come to believe that a fair average for the number of chicks in each brood that reaches maturity is four or, at most, five. If this belief is correct, then about seventy-five new birds will be added to the flock when the pairs come together once more after the long nesting season. This makes the covey now number about one hundred sixty birds, for there will have been some loss among the adults during the nesting season, as well as the heavy loss among the chicks.

How many birds can safely be shot out of a flock of one hundred sixty birds without reducing too much the productive capacity of that flock? This question must be asked by every hunter who enjoys his quail shooting and wishes it to continue undiminished. As I see it, there will be a loss of at least fifteen or twenty birds from natural causes suffered by such a flock through the fall and winter. Hawks will take some, while cats and other preying mammals will take others. Though sickness and old age will bring about the death of a number of the birds, probably it is the sick and the old of the flock that are most often taken by the predators. If the hunter takes no more than thirty to forty, there will still be enough birds left to maintain the flock. It must be observed here, however, that no two years are exactly the same for the quail. In some years, surely, there will be more than sixty young birds added to the flock, and in other years there will just as surely be fewer than sixty added. In the same way, the losses among the old birds will fluctuate. At times fortune will seem to run heavily against them and an unusually large number will meet with accidents. At other times the losses will be light. Under such varying conditions no exact figure, such as thirty or forty, can be set for each and every open hunting season.

The next point of interest to the hunter is the number of birds that he actually kills each time that he takes the field. A count, to be accurate, must include those in the bag, those killed but not found, and those hit but not stopped, for the great majority of quail that are hit die either of their wounds or in the jaws of some predator that has found them when they are too ill to make their escape. Most hunters are entirely unwilling to make a count of this sort each time that they come in from the field. A hunt which my son and I had in some very rough country in the fall of 1946 provides a good example of how many more birds are killed than are actually bagged. When I had hit my eighth bird, the legal limit for Valley Quail that year, I came in, and Ed, seeing me put up my gun, came in too. He had hit nine birds. We each had three quail in our bags. Of the five that I had hit and had not been able to retrieve, one I had killed dead, as the saying is, by a well centered shot, but I had not been able to find it. A second I had hit hard just before it started to curve around an oak tree. This bird also I failed to find, being unable to see where it came down. Two others had been dusted with shot but had not been killed instantly, and a fifth had been hit lightly.

It will be remarked at once by most hunters who read this record that I shot very badly on that day. I admit the charge, if the very rough country in which I was hunting is not considered. The important point, however, is that even though the unrecovered kills are not usually as heavy as this in numbers, I am still confident that at least one Valley Quail is killed and lost to every two that are knocked down and found. If this is so, few more than twenty quail can be bagged safely from our supposed flock of one hundred fifty birds. I know of no hunted flock of this size that has so small a percentage of birds taken from it during a single open season.

There is another reason besides overshooting for the diminution, in some cases annihilation, of our Valley Quail population—one that is so short-sighted and so stupid that it enrages me every time that I think about it. It lies in the activities of the ground squirrel poisoners, men sent out and paid by the state to work havoc among the ground squirrels. In the past, grain impregnated with thallium, a metallic poison very deadly to all forms of animal life, has been scattered far and wide. Usually, no effort has been made by the spreader to put out the bait in such a way that only squirrels could get it. I have come on it, for example, placed on old stumps, in rodent trails through the thin grasses, and on the mounds of the ground squirrel burrows in places ten miles and more from the nearest cultivated field and over a mountain range from the nearest house.

As is well known, Valley Quail and ground squirrels live on the same ground in many areas, especially in those bushy and weedy patches about grain fields. How many times, in both the open and the closed seasons, have we all come on little coveys of quail as they gleaned along the edge of such a field! This is the favorite place for the poisoner to carry on his trade. The certain results of this practice, short-sighted and stupid almost beyond belief, need no further elucidation. It is my considered opinion that no one should be allowed to set out poison anywhere except under the most rigid supervision and under the most carefully framed rules.

Considering the matter further, it seems to me likely that in some instances poison has been put out for the quail deliberately. There are cases where large flocks of quail have been very destructive to crops. This has been true of grapes in small vineyards, especially. Vegetable growers have complained to me that the quail have done much damage to their produce by spoiling its appearance. For the most part, farmers and ranchers like to have the quail about, and they feel that the birds are a real benefit to them because of the weed seeds and the injurious insects that are gleaned. When the damage becomes considerable, however, these men feel that steps must be taken to abate the nuisance.

Some ten years ago, some of the orchardists hereabouts became exasperated at the damage that the finches, grosbeaks and orioles were doing to the apricot and fig crops. The simplest means of destroying these birds seemed to be to put out drinking fountains filled with arsenic-tainted water. This was very effective. Two or three years after this, the magpies fifty or sixty miles to the north of us became so numerous that the ranchers in that area put out poisoned grain. This, too, was effective. As this is a hog-raising region, the experiment was not tried a second time for fear of doing deadly harm to the hogs. In Marysville three years ago, poisoned grain was put out widely to diminish, if possible, the huge flocks of blackbirds that had grown up about the rice fields. The year that this was done proved to be the poorest one for pheasants that was known to the pheasant hunters there. Many hunters, therefore, became convinced that, while the grain had been effective in checking the blackbirds, it had been almost equally effective on the pheasants.

Another cause of death to the quail is the diseases that are common to all barnyard hens, and that the quail about the barns contract from the unpenned hens. Some of these disorders are particularly deadly to the quail and are the bane of the quail breeder's existence. So deadly are they to penned birds that many men now raise their young quail on wire netting stretched a foot or more above the ground, just as is being done more and more with baby chicks in the poultry business. Chickens may react well to wire bottoms on their pens, but quail look sadly out of place in such a pen because they have so strong a preference for close cover immediately over and about them.

Quail hunters fall into several categories. There is, first of all, the sportsman. He takes the field as regularly as circumstances permit, in carefully organized expeditions. Sometimes these expeditions take up the whole day, but often—and this is especially true of quail hunting today—when bag limits are small, a morning or an afternoon is sufficient. When he comes home, he cleans and puts up his gun, and he does not handle it again until he is ready to hunt once more. There is also the boy equipped with a small-bore gun who rarely goes on a full-scale quail hunt for the simple reason that such an expedition is beyond his reach. This young man hunts spasmodically, whenever occasion offers, in the areas rather close about his home. He may clean his gun often, but he seldom or never puts it away permanently. Individually, he seldom kills many birds at one time, yet his score for the year may be an impressive one.

It happens that my home is on the outskirts of the town, in a residential tract where even small houses are likely to have an acre or two of land around them. Were it not for the tame cats gone wild, this would be an ideal place for small coveys of quail. At one time I thought that I possessed such a flock. I saw these birds almost daily on my lawn, where they came for greens. Once I counted eighty-one birds in this flock: thirty-seven hens and forty-four cocks. That winter they were still about during the holiday season and for a while after this, but then I saw them no longer. Some time after this, a neighbor told me that he had given a .410 gauge shotgun to his son as a Christmas present, and that now the boy had turned into a real hunter. "Why," said the man, a trace boastfully, "he comes in every morning before breakfast with a quail or two." His enthusiasm for his son's prowess with the little shotgun fell on deaf ears. As he talked on, I silently divided "a quail or two" into eighty-one. As I figured out the problem, less than two months would be needed for the destruction of my small covey. No wonder that they no longer appeared regularly on my lawn! It was some five years after this episode before another quail was seen in my garden. By this time the clever little hunter had graduated from the local high school and had gone to college.

This is not an isolated instance. Several times I have been told since then by other men that "Young Bill" always has two or three quail in the icebox. In semi-rural areas I believe that many boys hunt more or less all through the year, and that they keep the quail coveys in their respective neighborhoods down to the smallest numbers. Few of them are restrained by the law governing the closed season on the birds. A covey is seen as it rests bunched together under a bush, let us say; there is a hurried trip into the house, barn or garage for the gun; there is an explosion; and then the young hunter picks up with satisfaction the two or three birds that he has killed on the spot.

With more premeditation, there is much hunting of quail out of season by adults. A hunter does not like to admit this, I know, but it is a fact. Talking to the leading conservationist of this district one day, I was startled at being told with some asperity that "you hunters are the worst violators of conservation principles with whom we have to contend." Thinking over this disagreeable statement, I came to the conclusion that there was much truth in it. As a class, we hunters have grievously overshot the quail population ever since we took to the field. As a class, we have violated our game laws at will, just as we have done with all other laws that momentarily have stood between us and the fulfillment of some whim. I must sadly confess that leaders of sportsman groups sometimes have been as much at fault here as have been the rank and file of hunters.

What is the remedy for all this illegal shooting? More game wardens would be a help, but only a help. If there were ten wardens where now there is one, there still would be much illicit shooting. The only effective means I know for protecting the quail is so to arouse public opinion among hunters that the individual will believe that it is to his best interest not only to keep others from shooting illegally, but also, and more important, to restrain his own propensities in this direction.

As for the man who hunts within the law, his conscience is clear, of course. Even so, he must accept at least a part of the blame for the destruction of the quail which has gone on steadily. In another place I told of a hunt from which John and I came home with fifty quail. As I see it now, on that memorable day we must have taken from that huge flock at least seventy-five birds, and when the lost kills and the hit birds are counted in the score, it is likely that we took more than this number. No flock of quail, no matter how large, can long stand successive drains like this one, whether they are legal or not. The quail population of the state has decreased steadily under the system of bag limits and open and closed seasons for the simple reason that it has been overshot every year.

In 1946, with a greatly increased number of hunters taking the field, the daily limit was reduced from ten to eight birds. This reduction in the daily limit will not lower the total take for the year. If ten hunters take the field and each one of them shoots ten birds, the group will come in with one hundred birds. If, during the next year, twenty hunters kill eight birds apiece, their total will amount to one hundred and sixty birds. This hardly can be termed a step in the right direction—that of saving the quail from extinction.

At best, a game law is a compromise between what should be done and what can be done to regulate the shooting of men who are not too careful in their observance of any law, whether that law attempts to regulate the speed at which a motor car is driven on the highway, the consumption of alcoholic beverages, or the killing of game. It is foolish to look to the law alone for protection for our quail. Other means must be devised and perfected to go along with and to supplement the efforts of the wardens if our quails are to be saved from a fate similar to that meted out to the passenger pigeon less than a century ago.

Hunting, no matter where it is carried on, is a wasteful business because so large a part of the game that is hit is not recovered by the hunter. This is true of deer hunting and duck hunting, as well as quail hunting. And of all the quail hunting done in the United States, I suppose that that done in the western states is the most wasteful. In another place I have estimated that at least one bird is lost to every two that are retrieved. It would not surprise me to find that the figures of this estimate should be reversed, that is, that one bird is bagged to two that are hit and lost. Certainly this is true of careless hunters, and there are many of these abroad. When a hunter is following a rapidly moving flock of a hundred or more birds, he can hardly be expected to let the flock get away from him as he spends five, ten, or even fifteen minutes in search of a bird that he has knocked down in thick brush and, because of some intervening obstacle, has not seen exactly where it fell. In almost every instance of this sort, and there are many in every good shoot, the hunter looks about him for a moment or two, and then, failing to find the bird, he gives up the search and goes on after the flock. It is in situations of this kind that the westerner most often wishes for a good dog.

If dogs are to be used generally in western quail shooting, it is apparent to every hunter familiar with the sport in the arid hills that they must be used very differently than they are used in the South. For one thing, a dog must stay close to his master, almost at his heels, if he is to be of much real use. The dog that goes off through the brush widely is soon lost, or he soon becomes so worn out that he cannot go on. If a wide ranging dog comes on a covey of quail at some distance from the hunter, the latter probably will not know of the find because the shoulder-high brush, as well as the broken nature of the ground over which he is hunting, will completely hide his dog from him. If he is lucky, and if the quail are not too far away from him, he will hear the birds sputter when they become aware of the dog. If the birds move off silently, however, as they often do, the man will be entirely ignorant of their proximity.

The services of a good dog are most needed by the hunter when the shooting begins after the first rise. If man and dog are content to go through the brush together up to this point, letting the man do most of the work of locating the covey, the dog may be fresh enough to find and bring in bird after bird that otherwise would be lost. Once the birds of a covey have become thoroughly frightened, they are likely to lie fairly well to a dog. Yet it must be remembered always that these are birds that do not roost at night on the ground, that they elude their enemies not by remaining motionless, but by running and, when necessary, by flying; and so they will tend to move off from in front of man or dog very much as a pheasant in the same situation would do. As our coveys become more and more reduced in size, I believe that more and more men will take dogs with them when they go into the sagebrush.

It is surprising to see how helpless is the man hunting western quails who all his life long has relied on a dog to find his killed birds for him. He kills a bird cleanly, and then he cannot find it. Nine times out of ten, he does not know where to look for it, for he has failed to mark carefully the spot where he saw it last. When I read one such hunter's account of his experience with Desert Quail, I laughed aloud; for this man, in all seriousness, advised other eastern hunters going west to take with them bountiful supplies of white handkerchiefs. When the hunter thus supplied dropped a bird he began dropping these white flags in the near vicinity of the spot where he thought the bird had fallen, and in this way he did not stray away from the place. This hunter also remarked that it was foolish to use one's hat as a marker because, in a very few minutes, the neutral-tinted hat would be as surely lost as was the neutral-tinted dead quail. From my admittedly western point of view, this is one of the most amusing accounts of a quail hunt that I have come upon in a book.

The satisfactions that come to the quail hunter when he takes the field during the open season are many and lasting for, whether he fills his bag or not on any given trip, he has a fine day in the open, he has much zestful exercise, and, almost always, he sees much to interest him and to stir his imagination. Though much less publicized, there are equally great satisfactions awaiting the same man in the same fields and on the same hills if he will go out without his gun to see how the quail are getting along during the closed seasons. When he comes home from such an excursion, he will have no birds in his game bag, but his mind will be filled with pictures that hardly could have been his had he gone with a gun in his hands to hunt the birds. More than this, he will have gained an insight into the habits and the small traits of character of the birds that will be of great use to him later in the year. To illustrate this obvious truth I will set down but a single experience that befell another quail hunter and me one evening in Arizona when we went out to look for Desert Quail in a short, rough canyon near the New Mexico Line.

The canyon in question was shaped like a huge basin or bowl with its southern side broken out. Its bottom was almost level for a distance of a mile, and then its sides rose steeply to high and rough ridges. In its bottom grew a fine stand of suhuaros, the many-armed giant cactus of the desert, and between these extraordinary plants there were thick and high bushes of cat's-claw and many other spiny and thorny shrubs.

We went up the sandy wash in the bottom of the canyon because, not being in an army tank, this was the only practicable way through the clutching cat's-claw. There were quail in the brush on either side of us, but, for the most part, they kept to this thick cover and we saw only a bird or two as we moved forward.

Arriving at a point where the wash began to narrow and to rise more sharply, we sat down on the coarse sand in a place that commanded a good view both to the right and the left of us and prepared to wait in silence for the quail to come into the wash and to show themselves. A cardinal sang in the cat's-claw, and once or twice we saw it, a vivid flash of brightest red, as it flew from one perch to another. Overhead there were many white-winged doves flying from the top of one suhuaro to another and feeding on the fruit of the huge cacti. This fruit grew in tight circles or crowns on the tops of the arms of the suhuaros. Each individual fruit or "pear" was about the size of a small lemon and shaped like a tiny keg. The doves reached the centers of these "pears," whose sides were covered with clusters of thin, needle-sharp stickers, through holes pecked in the thornless flat tops.

We watched the doves with the greatest interest until, suddenly, we were aware of a movement in the wash a hundred yards above us. Looking that way, we were amazed to see the head of a Javelina, or wild pig, thrusting out from behind a boulder as the animal looked down the wash for signs of possible danger. Apparently it did not see or scent anything disturbing, for it stepped unconcernedly into the center of the bare sand, and then came slowly toward us. Almost immediately another Javelina stepped out from behind the boulder, and then another and another, until in a few moments there were some twenty animals in front of us. They were of all sizes. One sow was accompanied by two half-grown offspring, and another sow had under her two little fellows that seemed to be less than a week old.

For some inexplicable reason, they were wholly unaware of our near presence. Several of them began to root energetically in the soft sand, as though in search of water; the sow with the half-grown young flung herself down on the sand and allowed her offspring to nurse. The second sow continued to move slowly down the wash toward us, her two little ones running along under her. Watching them closely, it seemed to me that the babies kept in touch with their mother by erecting the hair on their backs and keeping it in contact with the hair on her belly, just as a trolley car is kept in touch with the live wire overhead by its trolley.

The trio came closer and closer to us, and still they were unaware of our presence. At last, at perhaps twenty-five yards, the mother sensed us, and she stopped dead in her tracks. Whether she had smelled us or seen us I could not tell. As she now stood looking at us, every one of the long hairs on her body was slowly lifted erect, and then curled forward. Then away she went for the security of the brush, taking the other members of the herd with her, a pig at a time, in strung-out formation. One of the babies managed to keep up with its mother when she first rushed away, but the other one lost contact after a step or two, and it stood bewildered and alone on the open sand. There was a tremendous commotion in the cat's-claw. Then, after the last of the herd had disappeared from our sight, but while their progress upward could be plainly heard, the agitated mother came back for her offspring. Seeing her, the little fellow dashed under her and made contact through the long hairs of his back; then the two went quickly into the safety of the brush.

When the noise of the running Javelinas had quieted to silence, and the wash had returned to its former stillness, we went forward to inspect the place where the pigs had been rooting. To our amazement, we saw that in the very short time that they had been at work, they had been able to root down to moist sand.

The memory of that pleasant evening, when we were looking for Desert Quail and came on so many other interesting forms of wild life, will remain in my memory, I am sure, long after many of the incidents of successful hunts have faded into nothingness. Happy is the quail hunter who has the time and the inclination to go out into the coverts at all times of year.